CW00742943

REAL AND REEL

The education of a film obsessive and critic

BRIAN MCFARLANE

Foreword by Bruce Beresford

For Geraldine and our family, with love

Other books by Brian McFarlane:

The Encyclopedia of British Film
The British 'B' Film (with Steve Chibnall)
Michael Winterbottom (with Deane Williams)
Screen Adaptations: Charles Dickens' Great Expectations
The Cinema of Britain and Ireland (ed)
Lance Comfort
The Oxford Companion to British Film (with Geoff Mayer and Ina Bertrand)
An Autobiography of British Cinema
Novel to Film
Sixty Voices: Celebrities Recall the Golden Age of British Cinema
New Australian Cinema: Sources and Parallels in American and British Film
   (with Geoff Mayer)
Cross-Country: A Book of Australian Verse (with John Barnes)
Australian Cinema 1970-1985
Words and Images: Australian Novels into Film
Martin Boyd's 'Langton Novels'

Published in Australia by Sid Harta Publishers Pty Ltd,
ABN: 46 119 415 842
23 Stirling Crescent, Glen Waverley, Victoria 3150 Australia
Telephone: +61 3 9560 9920, Facsimile: +61 3 9545 1742
E-mail: author@sidharta.com.au
First published in Australia 2010
This edition published 2010
Copyright © Brian McFarlane 2010
Cover design, typesetting: Chameleon Print Design
The right of Brian McFarlane to be identified as the Author of
the Work has been asserted in accordance with the Copyright,
Designs and Patents Act 1988.

McFarlane, Brian
Real and Reel: The education of a film obsessive
and critic
ISBN: 1-921642-58-0
EAN13: 978-1-921642-58-6
pp194

Acknowledgements

My thanks are due to friends who have read parts of this book at various stages of its lengthy gestation and for their encouraging comments. They include: Margaret Barker, Elisa Berg, Ian Britain, Jonathan Croall, Gavan Daws, Kevin Foster, Melinda Hildebrandt, John Johnson, Pauline Nestor, Brenda Niall, Neil Sinyard, Andrew Spicer and Jason Steger. I thank Jan Fox for access to John's letters, Tarquin Olivier, Steve Chibnall and Wendy Driscoll for help with photographs, the University of Melbourne Special Collections for images from issues of *Farrago*, and the Nhill Historical Society for enabling me to check back issues of the local paper and for photographic assistance. I am grateful too to the editors of *Australian Book Review*, *Meanjin* and *Metro* (ATOM), and Methuen (UK) for permission to reprint extracts. I also thank Kerry Collison, publisher at Sid Harta Publishers, Melbourne, editor Ormé Harris, for her vigilance, and Chameleon Print Design for type-setting and cover design, and Matthew Frost, publisher at Manchester University Press, UK.

Above all, in putting these recollections together, I am indebted mainly to my wife, Geraldine (aka Gerie), who kept persuading me to keep at the work. I think she was perhaps looking for explanations for why household chores so often seem to have had a low priority. And I must also thank my children, Duncan, Susannah and Sophie, for the many hours they spent in cinemas in their formative years when I probably should have been teaching them valuable skills. This book is dedicated with love to them all, to my sister Margaret, and to my children's families, including grandchildren who've looked to me for guidance in movie-going if not to more character-building pursuits.

Melbourne, 2010.

Foreword

I first met Brian McFarlane in Melbourne some years ago after writing him a fan letter because of his entertaining book *Sixty Voices* (published in 1992) — a collection of interviews with actors, producers and directors 'recalling the Golden Age of British Cinema'.

Brian has published notably on British cinema, a largely under-researched field until recent decades. He is not, as he points out in this new book, at all unaware of the delights of American and European cinema. He does, however, have a rare appreciation of those low-budget British films of the 1940s and 1950s that almost invariably showed in Australia, if at all, on the lower half of double-bills. I can't bring myself to agree with his admiration for the director Lance Comfort (Brian has actually written a book about this obscure figure), but fully endorse almost all of his other enthusiasms for so many sadly forgotten actors, writers and directors. I recall seeing *The Square Ring* (director Basil Dearden, producer Michael Relph) around 1952 — on the lower half of a double-bill — and being stunned by the accessibility of its characters. They were so *real*, unlike those in most American films of that era. Needless to say, Brian McFarlane is the only person I have ever met who has also seen, let alone written about, this neglected film.

I grew up in the — then rural — outskirts of Sydney and shared almost identical film-going, and not-going, experiences with Brian. I, too, had parents whose attitude to my film attendances varied from the *totally forbidden* (my mother once explained to me that films were suitable only 'for the servants' — although our housing commission house was devoid of this category of person) to the *barely tolerated* — allowing a once a week visit to the local (Toongabbie) school of arts-cum-movie theatre.

I am not meaning to imply that this book ('*not* an autobiography but merely a rather specialised memoir' — Brian explained to me in an email) is in any way esoteric. I also disagree with Brian that it is 'specialised'. His stories of his childhood and youth in the Victorian town of Nhill are vividly described and touching. The people — family and friends — are realised with perception and humour. His prose style is so precise and so incredibly witty that I found myself constantly laughing out loud — and I don't recall doing that since reading Waugh's *Put Out More Flags*.

Bruce Beresford

Introduction

Hurtling round the freeways bellowing along with Johnny Cash about 'That ring of fire', I'm made aware anew of how the movies may change your life. To the best of my knowledge I'd never consciously listened to the rockabilly king until early in 2006 when I saw *Walk the Line*. Now, a couple of years later and the proud owner of seven CDs featuring the country and western singer, driving has become a much more pleasurable — and a noisier — business for me, as Johnny and I, sometimes joined by his wife June, engage in rowdy duets or trios. This transformation mostly happens when I'm in the car alone, my family having some quite severe views about what they want to listen to or not. My dealings with Johnny and June, via Joaquin Phoenix and Reese Witherspoon's film incarnations of them, cast my mind back to how it started for me.

What follows is not remotely an autobiography, starting with how one's forebears arrived on the tall ships. There may be just 'a touch of the memoirs', as British actor Donald Sinden called his own reminiscences, and an attempt to sort out my dealings with the movies over the last sixty years. Writing it has led me to ponder how a childhood love can stay with you and grow over the whole course — personal and professional — of a life, particularly in the matter of turning me into a film critic and historian. If this is allied to a twin obsession with the printed word, it means that a great many of life's more pressing challenges have got nudged to one side. My nearest and dearest would, in this respect, probably point to, say, a haphazard approach to home maintenance, to little children being forced to know who Merle Oberon was before they could spell cat, and so on.

But perhaps even more than literature, the movies with their intense visuality, their capacity — and *need* — to show so much of the world's possibilities, can eat their way through your defences of reason and responsibility. I don't mean that they will lead directly to your becoming a cannibalistic serial killer as a result of seeing *The Silence of the Lambs*. No, I mean more insidious inroads into the ways you think, into your ideas of the beautiful or the horrifying or the wildly comic. They may not even lead you, as they did Mia Farrow in *The Purple Rose of Cairo*, to confuse the reel and the real. But my aim is to suggest how my sense of reality has been partly defined by what the movies have meant to me, how they have entwined themselves about the events and relationships and places that have made up a life, and how writing about them has been one of that life's most rewarding and persistent activities.

Chapter One
A very young film critic

I started writing film criticism when I was ten, mainly about films I hadn't seen, but I couldn't let that stand in my way. It wasn't my fault that I didn't see all the films I wanted to see, or, in fact, that I saw hardly any films at all. Further, I was writing for an uncritical audience of one: myself. Sadly — or, perhaps, happily — these juvenilia have not been preserved, but I do remember one telling judgement. Writing of *National Velvet* (unseen) and, knowing that Anne Revere (playing Elizabeth Taylor's mother) had won a Best Supporting Actress Oscar, I fearlessly designated it as one of the cinema's greatest performances, 'greater even than Marjorie Reynolds' [not sure if the apostrophe was there at the time] in *Dixie*', which I did see. Reynolds, a long-forgotten blonde beauty of restful demeanour, played her role mostly in a wheelchair and I was moved by how brave she was in the face of her disability and how selflessly she planned, near the end, to give up former fiancé and minstrel, Bing Crosby, to Dorothy Lamour. But sassy broad Lamour had a heart, too, and is left not only with Bing's devotion but also, as befitted her superior star status, the higher reward of giving him right back to brave and selfless Reynolds. Life and art were inextricably confused for me, and it would be a year or so before they were definitively differentiated.

If you grew up in north-western Victoria's Wimmera district, where, as far as the eye could see, the country was flat enough for ballroom dancing, you probably needed the stimulus of different terrains. There was nothing especially wrong with the Wimmera, but it did seem unvarying. Back in my unecological childhood, people hadn't noticed the attractions of the Little Desert, where flora and fauna would in later decades excite environmental attention. And back then, too, the solemn elegance of gumtrees wasn't widely appreciated. As far as I was concerned, 'scenery' stopped at the Grampians in the far south of the Wimmera. After that, it was acres of wheat paddocks, with towns interrupting the Western Highway roughly every twenty-five miles, and these in turn were separated by hamlets with a railway station and a silo. I don't doubt that there was more to it than this, but it didn't then seem to offer a landscape for the imagination to work in. (Possibly it was no more unrewarding an ambience than, say, Pauline Kael's childhood on a Californian chicken farm or James Agee's in the industrial town of Knoxville in Tennessee — and look where a passion for the movies took them.) Reading from an early age — and I can't remember a time when I wasn't — I came upon books that evoked mountains and gullies or villages full of quaint English characters or 'redskin' encampments or sea-swept adventures, and these fed an appetite that a little later would gorge itself on the movies and the worlds *they* opened up.

The first film I ever saw was called *Fighting Thoroughbreds*. We had gone for a holiday to Horsham from a tiny townlet called Lillimur, eighty miles further west. Whenever I've seen Lillimur since, it seems to be subsiding into the ground. I was six when we left there, my father having presumably decided that he was never going to have a farm of his own as distinct from working on someone else's, and, at his older brother's instigation, decided to go in for insurance at Nhill, thirty miles further down the railway line. Last time I saw Lillimur, in October 2008, I registered the disappearance of a school, three stores, a hotel, a bank, three churches, the 'Hall', the railway station and a tennis club, all of which were going concerns in my early childhood. I perhaps exaggerate when I use the term 'going concern' about the greengrocery and milk bar presided over by my father's Auntie Mary, a deserted wife of melancholy gentility, who was inventive in explaining the paucity of choice in her wares. Once, I remember, she had chocolates definitely scheduled for Lillimur, but the ship bearing them had been sunk by German enemy action en route. The tennis club with its four courts and modest clubhouse might never have existed. It was there that I first saw a grown woman in shorts, and on the c:drive of my mind is stored the greeting of the jovial minister, the Rev. Duffy, to this lady: 'So, Dolly, did you think we might be short of men today?' My parents' house, opposite the grave of the tennis club, was in surprisingly good nick but my grand-parents' much larger place (it even had a billiard-room) was now no more than a swelling in the ground. The council dam to which my mother recalled evening walks when she was pregnant with me had long since succumbed completely to Wimmera drought.

By contrast, Horsham seemed like a metropolis then, and for many years I regarded it as the last outpost of civilisation before the plains assumed unbroken sway. Of this first excursion to its Century Theatre I remember only two things. The first had nothing to do with the main film, but perhaps was in the supporting film of the usual double-bill or one of the previews. It was the face of an actress, Mary Treen, who was no beauty, but kind-looking — and sardonic. (I identified her years later via a still from *Casanova Brown* in a scene with Gary Cooper.) The second thing I recall is my Auntie Molly's buying us sweets in the shape of yellow bananas. Sixty-odd years on, the sight of those lollies, whose longevity in the confectionery market is surprising, never fails to recall to me that hot January Saturday afternoon — a sort of Proustian *madeleine manquée*. I am sorry to record that the Century not only has no blue plaque to mark my crucial first viewing but that it has entirely disappeared and is replaced by something called 'Hobbies'n'Tronics'. As to the film, *Fighting Thoroughbreds* was, for those who care about such minutiae, an outdoor piece about rival racehorse-owning families, and was made by Republic Studios, whose track record — as it were — left it many laps behind MGM or 20th Century-Fox, as I would realise several years on.

I can't say that the cinema instantly took hold of me at the age of five. Over the next few years, after we had moved from Lillimur to the more substantial Nhill ('means nothing to most people', I would in later years say wittily to people as I pronounced its name, which actually meant 'mist over the waters' in a local Aboriginal language), there were no more than a dismembered handful of matinees. (I've since heard of children in comparable towns who had matinees every Saturday, taking this *richesse* for granted.) All of these, to which my parents must have sent my sister and me to get us out of the way, seemed very alarming to me, and were shown at what was called 'The Theatre'. Its name was variously the Theatre Royal (1924), the Royal Picture Theatre (1927), the Nhill Memorial Theatre (1949) and finally (to date) the Nhill Memorial Community Centre. Among the matinee films I saw there were *Jungle Book* (*après* Kipling) in which I remember a forest fire that endangered man and beast alike, and *Gulliver's Travels*, an animated version by Max Fleischer of the Swiftian satire, full of fear-inspiring images. Most memorable from these very early encounters was *The Wizard of Oz*, which scared me witless, as tree-branches reached out to intercept Dorothy and her fellow travellers. Decades later, watching the film on video with grandchildren aged two-and-a-half and five snuggling up to me on a couch, I was amazed at their stoically cool reception of what had once terrified me. 'Just tell me if you get frightened,' I said comfortingly — and elicited no response. Calloused beyond his years, the five-year-old in question, on another occasion being shown *Lassie Come Home*, announced wearily to the room as Lassie made her arduous way back to the bosom of her former family, 'Grandpa's crying again.' Well, he'd already had access to filmed fictions in a way I could only have dreamt of at twice his age.

My situation changed one Saturday morning when my sister Margaret, a year-and-a-half younger, and I decided to write down the names of all the film stars we'd heard of. By this time I was already reading English comics called *Radio Fun* and *Film Fun*, unaware that I was feeding what would become a lifetime's obsession. Of course it meant that names like George Formby, Will Hay, Petula Clark, Laurel and Hardy, Abbott and Costello and Jack Warner were already known to me, so that we put them on the list. Even so, the list came only to seventeen and, to round it out to twenty, I made up a few. I remember thinking that 'Barbara Rye' sounded like a film star, and jotted the name down: it actually belonged to a member of Corinella's Sunbeamers' Club, a children's supplement in the Saturday edition of the daily newspaper the *Sun-News Pictorial*. I used to win certificates for 'colouring-in' pictures for competitions, and so did Barbara Rye. The Sunbeamers' pages also featured the adventures of an unregenerate young delinquent called Ginger Meggs, whose subversive activities I followed avidly. Pre- and post-1950 fans seem to have had access to 'swap cards' with film star portraits, but probably as a result of wartime paper shortages these didn't come my way, with the exception of one such card featuring a now totally forgotten actress called Sidney Fox, which some friend must have decided was of no further interest to him. Poor Sidney Fox, sad to say, died of a drug overdose when she was thirty-one.

I can't now recall why my sister and I should have been engaged in the list-making enterprise and certainly her enthusiasm for it failed to keep pace with mine. In the years that followed, when I needed every possible support for the struggle to get to the movies, I could only count on her partisanship if the film starred bobby-sox idol Van Johnson. All I can say is that somehow or other the movies must have filled a gap in my life. Being a swot who always came top in exams, small for my age, the youngest in my class, and not very good at sport, I obviously needed some other fillip to the imagination and film decided it would provide this for me. If you were brilliant at, say, football or playing the piano, that possibly took up the imaginative slack in your life. I can't remember what led up to that Saturday morning but what followed it marked me for life. About sixty years on, through all the distractions and delights of marriage, careers, children and, now, grandchildren, my feeling for the larger-than-life world up there on the screen, or even over there in the other corner of the living-room, is unabated.

But don't think it was easy. Unlike for some kids, children of my parents' friends even, there was no question of my being allowed to go to the pictures on a regular basis, scarcely even on an *irregular* basis. (Those matinees I mentioned earlier were rare exception and preceded my obsession with film.) My parents, admirable in many ways, such as giving my sister and me a secure childhood, feeding and clothing us well, taking us on holidays, tending us in illness — trivial stuff like that — had an entrenched suspicion of the movies' power to corrupt young minds if taken habitually. Their closest friends had a permanent booking for Saturday nights at the local theatre, and the children of those friends seemed to me immeasurably privileged. It can only have served my father right when, on the occasion of the screening of the multi-Oscar-winner *The Best Years of Our Lives*, he must have heard that this was a film to see and then had great trouble getting tickets and complained bitterly about the selfishness of other more foresighted people.

Dad loved laying concrete paths. As he went about disciplining the landscape with stark strips of cement, I was his unwilling helper from the age of about ten on. I usually wanted desperately, by this time, to get to the movies to see, as it might be, Abbott and Costello in *Hit the Ice* or Bob Hope in *Road to Morocco*; all right, my taste had yet to be fully formed. While my father was girding our house with his preferred substance, it was my job to keep him supplied with barrow-loads of bricks from a pile he'd had delivered to some distant part of the yard. As I was engaged in this infant exploitation (where was Lord Shaftesbury when I needed him?), I would keep up a running commentary about the need to get to the pictures that evening as a reward. To his credit, I suppose, he never hit me with a brick — or with a mallee-root on the Saturday when it was my task to move a pile of these brilliant fire-boosters from one side of a shed to another, presumably to satisfy some sadistic paternal whim. To be fairer now than I would have been then, I think I probably *did* get the reward I was so tiresomely negotiating more often than it seemed at the time. Not that you could ever be certain until the last minute. It was easier in winter to know if you were going to get your just deserts, because at about 7.30 you'd volunteer helpfully, 'Shall I get another bit of wood (or mallee-root) for the fire, Dad?' A clear 'No' meant, 'There's no need because we're going out shortly.' Have you ever heard more poignant accounts of infant aspiration and/or frustration?

I don't think my parents actively disliked the movies; they weren't 'wowsers' about them; they didn't know enough about them for that. It's not, either, that we were even picturesquely poor. My father was now a stock-and-station agent, on a reasonable enough salary; my mother didn't 'work' of course, but simply ran as much of the town as she could in various presidential and secretarial capacities. I don't think my parents were out-of-the-way stingy either, though I don't suppose there was much money to spare. For instance, I recall now that we never had an electric fan to blunt the effect of Nhill's ambitious summers or a radiator to do the same for its Spartan winters. But no, I can't claim anything very rigorous in the way of hardship, even though I was quick to point out any suggestion of under-privilege as it affected me, notably in relation to the movies. Somehow, obscurely, they just felt that the movies weren't 'good for' young children. As a result many epic battles were fought in the cause of seeing 'crucial' films, and this involved a lot of hard work, manual and psychological, on my part, only helped by my sister, as I said, if Van Johnson was starring.

On one memorable occasion, I was desperate to see a Columbia swashbuckler called *The Swordsman*, starring Larry Parks, who would be blacklisted by Senator Joseph McCarthy shortly after. Who now knows how, but I won the day and my father agreed. Did I at once say thanks? No, instead of being satisfied with this victory, I countered with, 'But this doesn't mean I can't go to *The Jolson Story* next week.' (Was the town in the grip of a Larry Parks festival?) My mother, normally more of a pushover, took me roughly to one side and said the maternal equivalent of, 'You're a fool. Why don't you quit while you're ahead?', though this would not have been an idiom at her command. What I wanted was an understanding that I would, like so many more privileged children of my acquaintance, go to the pictures *every* Friday or Saturday night without having to engage in long discussions or, worse, prodigies of infant labour.

So, what I didn't experience was that sort of kids-at-the-movies culture which seems to have been limited to larger towns and cities. There simply wasn't that opportunity to cut my teeth on the fare that typically made up children's Saturday matinees as a regular thing in such places. I saw the odd 'Hopalong Cassidy' somewhere along the line; it must have been one of the three 1943 items in the series, *Hoppy Serves a Writ, Bar 20* or *Colt Comrades*, because I remember Robert Mitchum was in it and I was able to identify him by the time I saw it several years late. This modest 'oater' may have initiated my life-long love of westerns, but I never knew a steady diet of such fare. Further, because we lived at a slight remove from the main part of town where the theatre was, we would not, in any case, have been allowed to go unaccompanied to the movies at night. This would have involved a walk home between the unilluminated recreation oval on the one hand and the dam attached to the flour mill on the other. There were, then, a few intervening years when we would go as a family, complete with rugs in winter as the theatre was quite unheated, before it was conceded that, on special occasions (i.e., when I'd won the battle), we'd be allowed go alone at night. Not until I was fourteen or fifteen, could I more or less count on getting to the pictures on a regular basis. By then, I could join friends at the theatre and I didn't have to be taken or collected. But though other kids went routinely, I don't recall 'the pictures' ever being a major topic of conversation. And by this time, too late for me to care much, there was a cliff-hanger serial shown each Friday night at 7.30. I don't think any of my age-group were holding our breaths about this from week to week, feeling it was a bit beneath us, but I can remember using it on the odd occasion when I felt the need for an extra argument for my getting to the pictures: 'It's a really important episode of the serial that I have to see ...'

Unlike any of the other kids as far as I recall, I wanted to *know* all about the films I was seeing: imaginative involvement with what I was watching wasn't enough for me. And unlike anyone else that I knew of, I stayed obsessed with films for the rest of my life. I suspect too that I was the only one who conscientiously recorded his keenly critical perceptions of the films he saw — and would continue to do so, in one forum or other, for a further sixty-odd years. James Agee, whom I came to revere when his reviews in book form (*Agee on Film: Reviews and Comments by James Agee,* 1958) came my way in the early 1960s, told his first readership in *The Nation* that he had been 'deeply interested in moving pictures, considerably experienced from childhood on in watching them and thinking and talking about them'. I didn't have that formative 'experience' and certainly didn't get to *watch* them often enough, but, when I did, I could certainly relate to his last phrase in the quoted sentence: I thought about them most of the time and talked about them whenever I possibly could nab a willing listener. Or even *unwilling* ones, as was more often the case, but that was their problem.

Looking back as dispassionately as possible, I don't think, apart from the matter of the movies, that mine was a childhood of marked deprivation; at the time, though, this seemed cruelty of a high order. We were taken to circuses, touring plays (Ronald Jeans' *Young Wives' Tale* caused locally a moral rumpus for its 'filthy' dialogue, but there was no problem with the Council of Adult Education's productions of J.B. Priestley's *Laburnum Grove* or Goldsmith's *She Stoops to Conquer*), the 'Blind Concerts' (i.e. in aid of the Melbourne Institute for the Blind) and so on. But the movies never won the same level of acceptance as a good 'live show'. It's not as if my parents were notably cultivated, so where was this prejudice, if that's what it was, coming from? In general, in those post-war years, it is probably true to say that the movies simply weren't taken seriously, though they were perhaps in some dim way disapproved of. They were essentially seen then, as they probably still are by many, as mere 'entertainment', whereas from a very early age they were for me a heightening and crystallising of what passed for life.

In spite of this affecting picture I've been drawing, in one way or other I did manage to see more films than it felt like at the time. On recently checking the pages of the *Nhill Free Press*, I found we had been to the pictures eight times in 1944, but that's not many if you're thinking in terms of addiction, is it? However, even at the rate of a handful or so a year, the total adds up. And certainly there were several key films in early years, key for me in the sense that they would have repercussions for ensuing decades of my life. For example, a child-and-dog film, *My Pal Wolf* (1945), struck me, in a very simple and direct way, with the difference between art and life. I was probably eleven when I saw this at a children's matinee, again in Horsham. A Hollywood 'B' movie, it is of little intrinsic interest, though it is competently made, of its kind. That is, it was a programme-filler which would normally have been the pre-interval half of a double-bill, when it wasn't being used as fodder for a kids' Saturday-afternoon programme. While her parents are engaged in 'important' war work in Washington, a little girl, Gretchen (Sharyn Moffat), is being neglected on their Virginia estate. Gretchen's mother engages an English governess, Miss Munn (Jill Esmond), to look after the child in the house with a lot of devoted, cosy retainers. Miss Munn takes one look at this lot (and the eponymous dog) and decides to exercise a firm hand. This may be the only kind of hand she has, and Gretchen's mum's failure to solicit reliable references has much to answer for.

The upshot is that Miss Munn alienated everyone — except me. What, I said to myself, is going on here? In real life, I'd find this woman oppressive, nasty and mean; in this film, though, I can't take my eyes off her. She seems so much more interesting than anyone else in it. In real life, I mean, I liked good people and still do — some of my friends are good people — and as the novelist Ivy Compton-Burnett has so wisely said: 'I think there is more to be said for good people than is commonly allowed'. What I think I'd stumbled on, though in no position then to articulate it, was 'the difference between art and life'. Meanness was so well delineated by Jill Esmond that I had no difficulty in suspending my years of moral training to prefer it to the spectacle of all those drab good people played by a lot of folksy character actors. For instance, we were meant to applaud a 'lovable' old character actor, George Cleveland, as handyman Wilson, who finally stands up to Miss Munn, saying: 'When you first come here, I didn' like you — and I still don't'. To this day, the spectre of Miss Munn hovers over my film- (and TV-) viewing. When, I wonder, did I last see a film where the goodies were more fun than their (usually better-scripted) opponents? More generally, though, *My Pal Wolf* taught me, at this early age and at some subconscious level, that our responses to filmed fictions don't have to mirror our ways of reacting to comparable real-life situations.

A *Song to Remember* (1945, Charles Vidor), a more or less unreliable biopic about Chopin and George Sand, made me a life-long addict of Merle Oberon's dark beauty. This addiction many years later took me to her palatial home in Acapulco. At the time, perhaps 1947 by the time it hit Nhill, it was perceived as a big prestige job that even *we* would be going to. It was humiliating to me that my father preferred the supporting film, a comedy called *Mama Loves Papa*, starring Leon Errol. Even more humiliating, in hindsight, is the fact that this may have been the better film. A *Song to Remember* had run for a year at Melbourne's Savoy Theatre, later given over to the cachet of foreign-language films, and it took its time getting to the west Wimmera. Most people of my vintage who saw it will immediately say when it is mentioned, 'Ah yes, the blood on the keys'. Chopin (played by Cornel Wilde), referred to as 'Showpang' as often as not, proves to have been a brave Polish patriot, who at one point, while performing at a grand dinner, leaves the piano and announces fearlessly, 'I do not play before tsarist swine,' and heads off to Paris, where by chance he runs into Liszt (Stephen Bekassy) in Pleyel's piano establishment, and they play a duet, back to back, on two pianos. Shortly afterwards, Madame Merle, in grey pants, red waistcoat, black cutaway and top hat, strides in — and won my adoration for the next sixty-odd years. She said little in this scene, but as she and Liszt move on to their own table she inclines her head to look provocatively at Wilde to say, 'I hope you will like Paris, Monsieur Chopin. I'm sure Paris will like you.' Simple words of courtesy maybe, but on Merle's lips charged with subtle sexual promise.

If the cast had problems pronouncing Chopin's name, this was nothing to the variants it offered on George Sand. But who cared? Certainly not barely-pubescent I. I thought I was not only in the presence of unparalleled beauty (and I still think that) but also of great art. 'No one knows this human jungle better than I. Whoever fought more bitterly to survive in it?' she challenges. 'All these years in the face of contempt and slander. To have some talent and ambition and to be a woman. In the eyes of men something slightly better than a head of cattle.' Her eyes flash, her colour heightens and her handsome bosom heaves as she levels these accusations at the gender-discriminatory treatment that has been her lot. (Why haven't the feminists lit upon this flare-up?) She whisks Chopin off to her island retreat ('You could write miracles of music in Majorca,' she alliterates) and, when she gets him there, later orders him to 'Stop that so-called polonaise jumble you've been working at for days,' and pay more attention to her. Well, all that driving rain does no good for his tubercular chest, but he insists on a fund-raising pan-continental tour for beleaguered Poland (an extended montage of trains, calendars and iconic structures) before the famous blood drips on the keyboard. As he lies dying, Merle is having her portrait painted and when his mentor, old Professor Elsner (Paul Muni), shuffles in to say that 'Frédéric has asked for you, Madame,' she answers, with not so much as a quiver of that peerless profile, 'Frédéric was mistaken to ask for me. Please continue Monsieur Delacroix.' In scene after scene, she commanded the screen and my youthful attention with beauty of a kind I'd never seen before — and scarcely since. A recent television screening of her 1941 film *Lydia*, in which she convincingly ensnares the love of three suitors, merely vindicated my youthful tastes, as did a still more recent purchase of *A Song to Remember* itself.

I shall return to Merle in a later chapter. It's enough to say here

that she established for me a standard of female beauty that has stayed with me. Never a gentleman who preferred blondes, I found that the actresses whose beauty I subsequently most admired were almost all brunettes like Merle (apart from the odd gorgeous redhead like Geraldine Fitzgerald or Rita Hayworth, and the occasional blonde of today like Scarlett Johansson). Among them were Ava Gardner, Googie Withers, Audrey Hepburn, Penelope Dudley Ward and, nearer the new century, Juliette Binoche, Daniela Nardini (of TV's *This Life*, and blessed with sensational legs) and Helen McCrory, most recently being a sharp but too attractive Cherie Blair in *The Queen* (2006). More important, I married a brunette who, as many noted at the time, bore a striking resemblance to Merle.

Films don't have to be good to change your life; they just have to strike something responsive in you as *My Pal Wolf* and *A Song to Remember* did for me. Mind you, at this stage of my film-going life, I found most films 'good' and was in no position to be picky. *And* they didn't have to be seen in the plushy purlieus of metropolitan cinemas. My early film-going was conducted in the local wooden-floored theatre, also used for concerts, balls, speech nights and other notable occasions. Kids could go for ninepence in the wooden seats, and, as I grew older and was there without parental supervision, I'd join others who had paid this sum and, as soon as the lights went down, we'd slink back to the first row of padded seats, Beryl, the usherette, turning a kind blind eye. In those days, sitting further back was a sign of class and/or financial discrimination. Some aspired to 'upstairs', where there may even have been carpet on the floor and where the 'best people' sat. The film-viewing culture of today, when people choose to sit very near the screen and have the whole thing wash over them, was several decades away. The 'Theatre' has now had a substantial face-lift and is called the Nhill Memorial Community Centre. It is still used for much the same activities, including balls, concerts and (sadly) only occasional film-screenings and the seating accommodation is limited to the swishily refurbished old 'upstairs' in recognition of declining demand. Back then, there were two separate programmes per week: one on Wednesday (when revivals were shown, along with other less prestigious titles); and another on Friday and Saturday nights. Unless the main film was very long, like *Captain from Castile*, or the three-hour *Since You Went Away* (Claudette Colbert keeping her exquisite chin up for the war effort), the programmes were all double-bills. The 'supporting film' was usually about an hour long and the evening was further extended with newsreel, trailers and sometimes a cartoon, while, on Friday evening in the late forties, all this was preceded by the half-hour cliff-hanger serial. Talk about getting your money's worth — if that's what you wanted for your money.

Others in small towns have no doubt had vistas opened to them by other stimuli; for me, it was the movies. Or to be more exact, the movies *and* the printed word. I was given books from the earliest age and they've been indispensable ever since: there were adventure stories (*Brothers of the Fleet* anyone?), school stories, invariably set in English public schools, Edward S. Ellis's dealings with 'red Indians' and a very few Australian-set tales, including Mary Grant Bruce's 'Billabong' series, which were set in a romanticised bush, and which were a legacy of my mother's own childhood. Fantasy took a header on a wet winter Saturday when I was thirteen. The local football team must have been 'playing away' and we hadn't gone and I was bored. Someone, perhaps a well-meaning teacher, had lent me a copy of the Everyman hardback (were there any other sort then?) of *Pride and Prejudice*; I began idly to read this unpromising-looking work, found nothing much happened but that I kept turning the pages nevertheless. If it wasn't much like one's own home-life, it seemed 'real' enough to be someone else's. I never willingly read fantasy again, and consequently have to spend a lot of time avoiding in-depth discussions between *aficionados* of *Lord of the Rings* and of the 'Harry Potter' industry. I was hooked on realism from that day on and have always tried to justify this narrowness by saying, 'I blame Jane Austen.' In 2007, I was asked to give a lecture at a Melbourne conference on Austen, and was at last able to use this evasion as a title.

Oddly, though, when it came to film I wasn't locked into realism with anything like the fixity of my reading preferences. I loved westerns (and easterns), epics, musicals, adventures, swashbucklers, war films, romantic melodramas (if there wasn't too much kissing), science-fiction, thrillers: the lot, as long as it was on a screen. (I even liked those church-hall lantern lectures that visiting bishops would show, depicting their sojourns among the heathen.) Tastes would change of course over the years, until, as I write, I realise my early predilection for literary realism has now more or less encompassed my film-viewing preferences as well. In other words, give me *Junebug* or *Jindabyne* any day over big stupid films like *Troy* or *King Arthur*, or the high-tech intricacies of *The Matrix*: in other words, the wheel that began turning in one medium now spins in another as well. Age, no doubt, has a lot to answer for, but this early preference has continued to produce serious gratification in the two media that have meant most to me — and, as I write, I realise that this bias has also spilled over into my tastes in art, spanning the centuries from Breughel to Edward Hopper.

From the very earliest stage, it was becoming apparent to me that I never wanted to be *in* films and that I had no urge to be creative in the sense of making, or being involved in the making of, films. This may be partly explained by my almost total lack of technological skills. I have emptied a room by showing the coloured slides I took to commemorate highlights of my first overseas trip. I can drive a car and use a computer without the slightest grasp of, or interest in, the underlying processes. Nor did I fancy myself as John Wayne or Bob Hope or anyone else; what I wanted to do was to *write* about them. Naked opinionatedness would later give way to more high-minded critical tenets but the delight in sorting out what pleasures the films were giving me was there from a very early age. As well, I liked to draw large, bold ads for favourite titles, privileging my personal favourites among the stars and, more unusually perhaps, the character actors I most cherished. Well, there was no point in writing about films just for yourself if you couldn't indulge yourself a little, was there?

Chapter Two
What deprivation can do for you

In my country town, all films arrived several years late, but, whereas Hollywood films would get there eventually, there seemed to be no such guarantee about their British counterparts. (Foreign language films were of course unheard of.) From one point of view the rarity of British films was odd: the cultural links between the two countries were then much stronger, and Australia was still much closer in spirit to Britain than to the US. We still celebrated Empire Day on 24 May at school; we would attend 'the Church of *England*' for several more decades; some people still spoke of England as either 'home' or 'the old country'. In Nhill, and I'm sure this was common, there was a committee called 'Food for Britain' in the post-war years, and my mother, like many others, kept up correspondence with the grateful recipients of tins of IXL peaches and other such Australian delicacies that were sent off to austerity-ridden Britain. Names were enclosed in the parcels and pen-friendships ensued: my mother had a long correspondence with a Mrs Chisnell, the headmistress of a girls' school somewhere in the north of England, and the insertion by my mother of my name in one such parcel led to an exchange of letters between me and a boy called Leonard Maxted, who had a strong interest in firearms which I wasn't fully able to share. From one of these 'Food for Britain' meetings, I remember my mother's bringing home the news that William McKell, Labor Premier of New South Wales, had been appointed the next governor-general, to succeed the Duke of Gloucester, who had proved a far from imposing figurehead. Nevertheless, some of the ladies had felt this was an insult to the royal family: not merely for the Duke to be followed by a mere Australian, but a Labor man to boot. Yes, pro-British feeling was still running high.

Most of the films I remember vividly from the post-war years were of course American. Perhaps the fact that I didn't see many may account for these having stayed with me. One was grateful for having people to stay if for no other reason than that they had to be entertained in some way. The choices available were so restricted there was always a chance of getting to the pictures under the umbrella of hospitality. Looking back, and recalling that adage about what happens to fish and house guests after three days, I wonder how we could have borne having people, usually relations, to stay for weeks at a time. I remember still with distaste one unlikable cousin arriving with his parents, showing me his substantial collection of Wrigley's chewing-gum packets, and explaining that he wouldn't be able to offer me one because he had them carefully calculated to last the three weeks of his stay. However, it was to such invasions that I owed sightings like those of: *Easy to Wed*, a lavish MGM musical with Esther Williams and my sister's idol Van Johnson, a remake of the superior *Libelled Lady*; the Australian rarity, *Bush Christmas* with Chips Rafferty and a bunch of cattle thieves; and *Mrs Parkington*, a multi-generational saga of American upward mobility, with Greer Garson blowing a provocative kiss-curl off her forehead well into old age. And there was Greer again, inventing radium as *Madame Curie*, to which Mr Miller, our science teacher, encouraged us to go for its educational value, as I pointed out to my sceptical parents. I didn't care *what* pictures I saw, as long as they moved.

Speaking of Mr Miller reminds me of how well I think I was taught at this country high school. It sounds wet, I know, but there is scarcely a teacher whom I don't remember with some gratitude and indeed affection. Even in primary school, unforgettably, at 10.30 every morning in primary grades 5 and 6, Mr Reynolds read *David Copperfield, Oliver Twist, Alfred the Great, Treasure Island* and (unseen since) *The Emperor of the Ants* for half an hour. Dickens, the great serial-writer, would have approved of the anticipation built up by these daily readings. I've never forgotten how, after reading the Artful Dodger's introduction of Oliver to Fagin and saying of him, 'He's from Greenland,' Mr. Reynolds asked us what we thought this meant. Always tediously eager to oblige, I suggested it meant he was cold. Could the actual explanation about naivety that followed have been my introduction to metaphor? Mr Reynolds was also the first person I'd ever come across who'd been to England, and his accounts of his travels probably initiated my life-long Anglophilia. We stayed in contact for the next forty years, until he died.

Mr (Bill) Head, tall and balding, taught us to sing operatic arias such as 'Up and guard the Nile's sacred shores' from *Aïda*, Purcell's settings of 'Full fathom five' and 'Come unto these yellow sands', and I first heard Ben Jonson's name in connection with 'Drink to me only with thine eyes' in a subject just called 'Singing' in what was then called Form 2 (now Year 8), all of which must have seemed pretty *recherché* stuff in the later 1940s Wimmera. Miss Waller, a witty, frizzy-haired woman whom I sometimes saw again years later (when I was forty-five she invited me to call her Pat, and I regarded this as a serious compliment), and Mr (Les) King, reserved and dignified, were exceptionally sharp and inspirational English teachers, opening up *Julius Caesar, Macbeth*, traditional ballads and Regency Poets, along with many other big names, to anyone ready to receive them. Mr King also lent me *Gone with the Wind* when I was fourteen and it was far and away the raunchiest thing I'd ever come across, though I barely understood what kind of establishment Belle Watling was running and why it was a bad thing for chaps to have been seen there. On graver, more life-determining matters, how many people under sixty now know the difference between nominative and accusative case? I do, because pretty, plump Miss (Ruth) Carne taught it to us in Form 1 — and I can't tell you what a boon it has been to me. Just think of all those writers who routinely use 'whom' because it sounds posher when it's really 'who' they need.

Back to visitors. There was a young married cousin of my mother's, with whom Mum was finding conversation a bit stilted but who was mad about the movies, and I won considerable favour with both women for talking interminably to this rather indolent young visitor. She in turn was instrumental in getting me to see *The Rake's Progress*, which in later decades I'd learn to regard as a minor masterpiece, and the irresistible Technicolor musical, *Meet Me in St Louis*, which I still think of as one of the most-nearly perfect films ever — in the same week! When we weren't having relations to stay, in our civic-minded way we had an elderly married couple called Hardingham, in residence for ten days, for three meals a day, for the Back-to-Nhill celebrations. They took us, as well they might, to see *Broadway Rhythm*, in which a beauty called Ginny Simms sang unforgettably — well, *I* never forgot it — Jerome Kern's 'All the things you are'. I was thirteen at the time and I didn't see it again for fifty years and was very impressed with my teenage discrimination when I did. I always disliked knowing that she was reputedly the object of the lustful attentions of her MGM boss, Louis B. Mayer, and am sure she resisted them. As my mother took ill during the 'Back to' celebrations, probably the result of her efforts relating to their organisation, the Hardinghams had even more reason to indulge my sister and me, and to their credit they did. They (he rather soldierly, she more earthy: had he met her in a canteen somewhere?) also took us, again in the same week, to see Joan Fontaine as *Ivy*, the wickedest woman in London, cutting a swathe through its unsuspecting menfolk. I interviewed her several decades later and she tried to convince me it was really a 'B' movie, but to no avail. There were very few beautiful murderesses in Nhill in those days, and I'd be surprised if there are many even now.

There were dog-and-child and horse-and-child films such as *Lassie Come Home* and its sequels and *My Friend Flicka* and its ditto; the only Australian films of these early years, *Bush Christmas*, the children's adventure, and the Kingsford-Smith biopic *Smithy*; a genuinely eerie ghost story, *The Uninvited*, to which my parents, characteristically ignorant of what might have been appropriate film fare for their young, took us; there was Bob Hope, whom my father genuinely enjoyed, so that the Saturday afternoon persuasions were less arduous than otherwise when, say, *Louisiana Purchase* or *Road to Morocco* were screening; and there was *The Bells of St Mary's* (well, what could sound more innocuous? — and was). And there was the odd glorious Western, like *Canyon Passage*, in which J. Arthur Rank hoped to make an international star of British Patricia Roc, but, with sultry Susan Hayward also in the cast, little Patricia hardly got a look-in, and she had finally to relinquish Dana Andrews to Susan. I never forgot the first image of the 'redskins' emerging dangerously from an Oregon forest to wreak harm upon hard-working settlers. There was, too, the black-and-white beauty of John Ford's *My Darling Clementine* (arriving three years late in 1949) with Henry Fonda as Wyatt Earp, and Linda Darnell bravely taking a bullet intended for someone else. I was always very moved by women behaving in this selfless manner, and am not sure that women in today's films are making such sacrifices for their menfolk. John Ford would go on to be the hero of my mature years, and his great Western, *The Searchers*, 1955, remains top contender for my all-time favourite film. No doubt there were others in these meagre but formative years, but these titles give some idea of the limited range that came my way while I was still at the mercy of parental whim.

One of the others was the first British film I ever saw, years after its topicality had passed — its title, *The First of the Few*, was prophetic for me. Perhaps because we always hanker for what we can't easily have, I became fascinated with the idea of British films. The few I did see came to seem exotic and they stayed in the mind, partly for their rarity, partly for personal reasons. This interest was fanned by the reading of genteel film journals called *Picture Show* and *Picturegoer*, which would arrive at Miss Ruby Dickinson's newsagency three months after publication date. Very poorly paid as I was (a fact I often mentioned to my parents), these fortnightly and, later, weekly publications, at threepence and later fourpence each, took most of my resources. They made me realise that, whereas it was available to me to be corrupted by, say, Betty Grable of the long legs insured by Lloyds of London because of their importance to wartime morale, I wanted to be corrupted by a better class of person. Such as, for example, Jean Kent, whom I read about as *Good-Time Girl*. What exactly *was* a good-time girl? I knew there was more to it than just having fun because it seemed she ended up in gaol. I don't think there were any good-time girls in my country town; certainly not in the Country Women's Association or Ladies' Guild with my mother. I did wonder if a good-time girl was something like a rather heavily-rouged young woman whom I once heard my mother describe as 'common'. There wasn't a hope in the world of such a film coming my way — or of my being allowed to go to it if it had. Or to the notorious *No Orchids for Miss Blandish*, if it had ever come to town. Some well-meaning busybody would have alerted my parents to the unsuitability of these racy entertainments for so young and impressionable a mind — possibly the local librarian, Miss Lil Shuncke, who once accosted my father in the street saying, 'Brian's been trying to borrow *The Razor's Edge* again.' So I had, having read about the film in the pages of *Picture Show*. Somehow (visitors again?) I got to see this corrupting work on film and have never forgotten that sumptuous beauty Gene Tierney descending the stairs as she prepares to go off for one more gaudy night with Tyrone Power before renouncing him in favour of John Payne for reasons of security. I now think, though, she might just as easily have decided she couldn't bear a lifetime of listening to the Power character's philosophy ('You can't *not* ask yourself what it all means,' he anguishes soulfully at one point). Miss Shuncke's library was a modest affair, with larger sections headed 'Mystery', 'Romance', 'Westerns' and a very small shelf labelled 'Literary Merit': I was chiefly looking for books which I knew had been made into films, hence my quest for the decadent Maugham title.

Another hopeful source of cinema-going was when my mother was 'on the dance'. That meant that she and two other members of the C of E Ladies' Guild were on supper duty for the Saturday night dance held in the church hall and a godsend, as it were, for the Anglican funds. The dance had been initiated during the war to entertain RAAF personnel stationed at the aerodrome but was maintained post-war for many years because it was so lucrative. It was scurrilously claimed that any young woman who didn't nab a husband, preferably an airman, from attendance at these dances during the war, either wasn't trying or was simply hopeless material. Unlike other vestrymen, my father was an asthmatic and was therefore unable to do the door duty of taking two shillings from customers. This was because the floor was treated with some sort of dust-making powder to facilitate dancing but which brought on Dad's asthma. As a result we would sometimes be taken to the pictures so as to collect Mum from the scene of this Saturday-night dissipation after the supper had been served. That's how we got to the tough war film *Immortal Sergeant*, the teary British musical *The Rose of Tralee* and the Ealing fantasy *The Halfway House*. For two shillings, patrons could dance for four hours to the piano played by Mrs Elsie Madeleine Watson (I thought 'Madeleine' sounded like a film star's name) with son Frank on the drums (or drum), and stuff themselves with sandwiches and cakes. In my mid teens, I got the job of sweeping the church hall next morning in time for Sunday school, in return for five shillings, which was a very substantial addition to my cinema-going and journal-buying needs.

In the matter of British films, my experience is a striking instance of what deprivation can do for you. I *longed* to see those films that Lionel Collier in *Picturegoer* or the unnamed critics of *Picture Show* would praise. They did justice to the Hollywood output, but their innate patriotism — chauvinism, even — would often lead them to extol the realist virtues of the home-made product. And in hindsight, I think they were right to do so: perhaps my life-long addiction to British films wasn't just a matter of these being so rare in my young life but also that, just as I was becoming infatuated with the movies, British cinema in those post-war years was enjoying a prestige it had never had before — and, arguably, has never rivalled since. The late forties (certainly 'late' in upcountry Victoria if these films arrived at all) saw the efflorescence of David Lean's Dickens adaptations, the ascendancy of Carol Reed and Anthony Asquith, and the maverick genius of Michael Powell, and many others. I remember it was a lay-down misère getting to *Oliver Twist* ('It's a classic Dad; we've read it at school') and, as for *The Red Shoes*, what could have sounded more respectable than the ballet? My mother had been on some women's outing to see Carol Reed's *The Third Man* one Friday evening and hadn't cared for it because there was too much running about in sewers, and I feared momentarily for my chances on the following Saturday evening, but in the event all was well and I saw what is still for me one of the most seductive films ever made. I doubt if I could watch those first two or three minutes with the voice-over talking about the 'old Vienna' and 'the classic days of the black market' as a body floats past, without surrendering to the ensuing two hours. I felt my youthful taste was confirmed when it was recently voted the most popular British film ever in a poll conducted by the British Film Institute.

There wasn't much in the way of British film after *The First of the Few*, a stirring account of the later life of R.J. Mitchell (played by Leslie Howard, who was killed shortly afterwards as he flew to Lisbon), designer of the Spitfire, arriving, as I said, some years after its wartime relevance had passed and several years after the death of its famous English-gentleman star. On recently checking the copies of the *Nhill Free Press* for 1944, I found there were ten British films screened in 1944 and sixteen in 1945, out of a possible (roughly) 180, and I'm including 'supporting' films and 'revivals' in these figures. The British films I saw were so rare as to have stayed in my mind for decades. There was a lachrymose semi-musical called *The Rose of Tralee*, dated 1942 but not seen till at least four years later, and very moving I thought then. I was always on for 'moving', as it made me feel I was in the presence of higher art. The British films I did see stayed in my mind sometimes for purely personal reasons. On one occasion I remember being at a Saturday-afternoon birthday party and storming out seething about some injustice, when my sister, also there and no doubt embarrassed at the stir I'd caused, came running after me to say she'd tell me a secret if I'd just come back: that she knew we were going to the pictures that night (Mum was 'on the dance') and the film was *The Halfway House*, a strange British fantasy starring Glynis Johns and her father Mervyn, about which I'd been making a tiresome fuss. I returned to the party and my behaviour was impeccable from then on. Even more potently, I still remember *The Seventh Veil* as the first film my sister and I were ever allowed go to alone at night, on condition we didn't leave the theatre during the interval to go into the street after ice-creams and the like. Well, we did. And we were caught. By our parents who were checking up on us. Even now, all these decades later, I still find that lack of trust hurtful. It makes you question the whole basis of family life.

But the film that really changed my life by getting me hooked on British films was neither a prestige job nor a scandalous corrupter, like any of those referred to above. They all came later. The film that was a watershed for me in this respect was to one side of either of those extremes. In perhaps 1947, having badgered my father into taking us to see *A Thousand and One Nights*, an absurd Eastern-set extravaganza which I had raised quite a lot of Cain about needing to see and which I've felt no need to see again in the decades since, I found I was greatly struck by the supporting film. This was in the days when we got two films for our money, and the film before the interval on this particular occasion was a British film called *Great Day*, arriving in up-country Victoria several years after it was made and, as with *The First of the Few*, years after its topicality had passed. Never mind, I was greatly struck by this busy, gently abrasive account of life in an English village singled out as representative of the British women's war effort and to be honoured by a visit from Mrs Roosevelt. The central character was a former World War 1 captain (Eric Portman) for whom peace has held no challenges; he makes life difficult for his wife (Flora Robson) who is a pillar of the Women's Institute; his daughter (Sheila Sim), in love with a dashing soldier in World War 2, influenced by her mother's unhappiness, has got herself engaged to an unromantic but prosperous, middle-aged farmer; and there's a suicide attempt before the end. Then, as a black car bearing the distinguished guest hoves into view, the whole village is assembled and 'Jerusalem' swells on the soundtrack. It's a moving ending, and still seems so, not because all the problems raised have been solved but because we carry away the various kinds of pain they have created, and because of its sense of people being united in a common cause that transcends the personal. It seemed to me as a child strikingly different from the American films I was used to and loved: it felt fresh, sharp and truthful in ways I wouldn't have been able to articulate then, and fifty years later it is still very much a film worth looking at. Indeed, Sue Harper, a recent film historian, has described it as 'quite simply a masterpiece'. And in 1999 I was very gratified to publish a small book about its director Lance Comfort, who seemed to me a neglected figure and who became one of my

*Eric Portman and Flora Robson as Captain and Mrs Ellis
in* Great Day *(1945)*

heroes in British film. His production-manager son John Comfort became a friend and we still exchange cards at Christmas.

This difference from the Hollywood style which had really conquered the world by the end of the 1910s — and the world on the whole had offered little resistance to the conquest — was not all that easy to pin down but it *was* palpable. Why *did* British films seem so different to me? Perhaps in that post-war world there was a sense of shabbiness about life that it would take a decade to get rid of and this was something Australia shared, though to a much lesser extent, with Britain but which Hollywood seemed unaware of. Growing up in the post-war world, such British films as I saw always seemed closer to my sense of the real world than American films did. The processes of Coca-Colonisation were not yet fully in place in Australia. In some ways the British films opened up a world of the *possible*, whereas the immensely efficient products of the Hollywood system, however much you admired — even idolised — them, seemed to belong to a different order of being. I knew quite early that I was never, for instance, going to be a courageous detective pursuing lost men and loose women down the mean streets of the post-war world of Hollywood thrillers; I would never be able to sing and dance like Gene Kelly, in or out of the rain; or become a town-tamer in the outback in the manner of, say, Randolph Scott or John Wayne out West. These glittering beings were not bothered by the minutiae of everyday life, which was what so many British films seemed to suggest life was *really* about. The way people lived in British films kept striking notes you recognised from daily living: you might just conceivably have been a member of the bike club in *A Boy, a Girl and a Bike* (imagine the ingenuousness of a title like that!) or been glad of the avuncular police protection afforded by P.C. Dixon (Jack Warner) in *The Blue Lamp*; your father might have been a farmer like the one in *Great Day* or gone for a drink at a pub like the one in the same film, and your mother might easily have been a force in the Women's Institute, often being similarly employed in her own territory.

Now, *Great Day* was never shown, in Australia at any rate, as other than a supporting film (it preceded the US *film noir* drama *The Locket* on the programme at Melbourne's Plaza cinema), but this reinforces my point about how certain films caught me unawares, and changed my perceptions not only about the movies but about life at large. They didn't have to be masterpieces to do that. One result was that whenever I got to Melbourne for holidays at this time, when I was about fourteen or fifteen, I would bend every effort to seeking out those cinemas that showed nothing but British films. One was the Athenaeum in Collins Street, now a live theatre where the rock musical *Hair* was once performed in a way that would surely have shocked Anna Neagle, the star of *Spring in Park Lane*, the first film I ever saw there in early 1949. (My father 'shouted' my sister and me and two cousins for two shillings all up on a Monday morning and felt he'd had a bargain.) The other was the Grosvenor (formerly more eclectically programmed as the Central), in Little Collins Street, behind the classy old store, George's, and there was a great double-bill there during the same holiday: the famous Ealing comedy, *Passport to Pimlico*, 'supported by' (as the term was) *Man on the Run*, a nifty British thriller with *film noir* perceptions of a deserter fleeing detection. Or later that same year a toothsome double-bill of *Sleeping Car to Trieste*, a spy adventure starring good-time-girl Jean Kent, and the family comedy, *Here Come the Huggetts*. Double-bills were a bonus to one who so much wanted to be acquainted with all these British films and actors he kept reading about — and about which he would later so endlessly write and broadcast.

Reading about film was a limited but voraciously pursued activity in those benighted days. My bibles were *Picture Show* and *Picture-goer*, and the fact that they arrived three months late by sea from Britain, to be distributed on a fortnightly basis by a Melbourne firm called Gordon and Gotch, was of no consequence to me. ('Your "books" have arrived,' Miss Dickinson would tell me.) It was not as if I was going to see the films they wrote about for at least two years or, in the case of the British films, longer — if at all. I can't over-estimate the influence of these two journals in my young life. They were due to arrive at Miss Dickinson's on Wednesday and I would cycle frantically (well, as frantically as you could on your father's reconditioned Malvern Star bike) at lunch-time to collect my 'books'. Sixty years later, I can still see in my mind's eye on what part of the page a particular film was reviewed, or indeed what films were reviewed in the issue of *Picture Show* on the cover of which Rita Hayworth was depicted, flanked by Gene Kelly and Lee Bowman, in *Cover Girl*. *Picture Show* had a lot of sedate 'gossip' about 'Filmland', mainly about who was going to be appearing in what new films, with occasional items about who had married whom. Less formal relationships were never mentioned, and indeed I did not know they existed in life itself. It also had pages of pictures from new releases in London, and all other releases were recorded with cast lists, many of which I memorised and some of which I can still repeat, though it is hard to find an audience for such a recitation. And for each film there was a brief review where I learnt words like 'competently' and 'efficiently', attached to other words like 'acted' or 'directed'. There was a major 'biography' in each issue, a discursive article, about such matters as the endemic use of flash-backs, or how 'Crime DOES Pay Producers', a page for fashion which I ignored, and a list of actors' birthdays for the relevant fortnight.

There was actually more reading in *Picturegoer*, and, in those days when films weren't being taken very seriously in journals, it offered not only ampler reviews ('SHOP FOR YOUR FILMS, with Lionel Collier' — if only, I used to think) but reflections about directors as well as stars, Hollywood and British studio news. It was in Collier's page that I first came across, in relation to some melodrama, the word 'transpontine'; if you don't know what it means, your childhood was even more deprived than mine. And what about 'peripatetic'? How many of you had come across that at age ten? These indispensable aids to my education made, as I said, a severe dent in my inadequate pocket money, especially when they both went weekly in 1949, causing me to seek employment outside the home. Wartime paper shortages had reduced them to fortnightly publication; apparently the paper was needed for making ammunition, in a way not wholly clear to me. Years later, when I was married and my parents were moving from the house I'd grown up in, my mother, not normally very forceful, made it clear to my new wife that, having taken me on, she had also inherited these boxes of *Picture Show* and *Picturegoer.* Neither mother nor wife ever valued these frail treasures as she should have, but, when I am gathered, my children should sell them on eBay. They will never need to work again.

As well as these two cherished and ultimately tattered publications, many of which I still have, I had to rely on the film 'critics' in the various journals and papers that came into our home. For some reason, we'd stopped getting the *Age* and gone downmarket with the *Sun*, and whoever was delivering the latter refused to go any further than a house a block away, so in all weathers and in the dark of night I would go to collect it from this house, making my way unmolested past the recreation oval (what were my parents thinking? the negligence is quite shocking), and stopping under the one street lamp to read the list of films showing in Melbourne and, on Monday nights, the reviews. The pathos of this undersized lad braving the elements and who knew what other dangers still seems affecting to me. Because a teacher had suggested that the now long-defunct *Argus* had at weekends an improving section for students, I managed to get this into the home, though my real aim was to read its extended film reviews. As well, the *Nhill Free Press* regularly ran brief pieces about the films that were being shown. Checking these recently, I found that *The Amazing Mrs Holliday* revealed songstress Deanna Durbin 'as an outstanding dramatic actress' (22 June 1944), while *Road to Morocco* drew praise as 'one of the funniest films ever designed to improve the nation's morale'. (11 November 1944) But I also noticed that almost all such 'articles' in the latter forties, all unsigned, were devoted to MGM stars and starlings such as Lana Turner or Robert Walker or June Allyson. Was there some sort of sinister collusion going on between Nhill and Louis B. Mayer that we knew not of?

The other sources of criticism, to use the term loosely, were the *Listener-In*, forerunner of today's *Green Guide* or *TV Times*, setting out the radio programmes for the week, and with a section headed 'Axes and Orchids' in which listeners would record their views on the latest offerings, and my mother's journals. Of the latter, the *Australian Women's Weekly* was the most notable. Previously, its main attraction for me had been the adventures of 'Mandrake, master magician, Lothar, his giant Nubian slave, and Narda, Princess of Cockaigne' as they were always announced. However, once the film obsession was underway, it was touch and go to which I'd turn first: Mandrake or the quite generous coverage of films, with reviews, gossip (again not the personal kind), and a couple of pages of pictures (quite handsome portrait shots of stars — this was where I first saw the beauteous red-haired and green-eyed Geraldine Fitzgerald — and an illustrated account of a new film). Looking at some of these reviews sixty years on, I must say that I could have cut my teeth on much worse. If they were not profound, equally they were not stupid, and were even quite outspoken. A film called *Rhythm Serenade* was dismissed thus: 'Vera Lynn's second film is an even drearier effort than her first…[with] a phony fairy-tale script of war-workers, the Merchant Navy, and general heroism…'(6 January 1945) The *Woman's Mirror* usually had a star on the cover, with a very brief biographical note inside, but was of otherwise no interest to me, except for the recurring comic-strip adventures of the Phantom (aka 'The ghost who walks'). In retrospect, I think it must be said that both Mandrake and the Phantom led their girlfriends on quite shamelessly, with never a hint of marriage as Narda and Diana, respectively, trailed round after these oddly accoutred chaps in all manner of dangerous (and, I now think, quite compromising) situations.

The *New Idea*, bearing no resemblance to its present-day incarnation with its assiduous attention to the doings of Brad and Jen and Angie, had a central double-page devoted to the movies. Even then this seemed to me superficial compared to the in-depth coverage of the *Women's Weekly*, let alone *Picturegoer*. Still, it was all grist to my mill and I just soaked up whatever information I could find, never for a moment doubting its accuracy or questioning its provenance. And without doubt my early writing about film was much influenced by the critical 'voices' I heard in the pages of these newspapers and journals. As for *The Listener-In,* its reviews were a little more substantial than those in *The Women's Weekly,* but they followed much the same pattern with a summary of plot (quite early on, I realised this wasn't what I most wanted from them), though it was more likely to account for its judgments. On Clarence Brown's *The Yearling* (1947) for instance, the reviewer opened with: 'The screen tells many good stories without much depth of feeling, and only an ordinarily good film results. But when it succeeds in telling a good story with genuine warmth and sympathy for its characters, you get such a film as *The Yearling'.* The review ends with 'This is a film with spirit. Throughout, it maintains an atmosphere of yearning for deep affection, and futile struggle against it, and against the pain that is inseparable from it'. (1-7 February, 1947) As I say, there could have been much worse starts for a would-be critic.

In the late forties I had weekend and holiday jobs, possibly as a result of my father's intervention. First was in an electrical goods shop, where my native ignorance of all things technical hardly stood me in good stead on the occasions when I was left in charge. Then came a milk bar/café where I spent a lot of time dusting chocolates below counter level and eating free ice-cream, as well as having on the premises a very typical country-town-café lunch of steak and eggs, chocolate sundae and milkshake every day and in consequence being paid at a rate no union would have countenanced. Finally, I became a 'smart lad', which was how the job was advertised when I left to go to university, at a grocer's where the perks were fewer — just the odd biscuit, pickings from Arnott's Assorted Creams — but the salary was better. The purpose of these stimulating employment opportunities was to make me more financially independent in the matter of getting to the pictures regularly. There was still the crucial matter of permission to be obtained but I began to get a feeling of wearing down my father's opposition. He'd make a token stand every now and then, but his all-but-total ignorance of the movies left him less well-placed in argument. 'I'm studying the book, Dad, so I need to see this' or 'Mr So-and-so [teacher] has recommended it, so I think I should go' or, desperately, 'Margaret particularly wants to see this.' Nevertheless, I think much of my determined character was formed, for good or — as many might say — ill, by the sorts of battles I joined in behalf of so crucial a cause.

One last episode comes to mind. I wanted very much for reasons now lost in the mists of time to see a film called *Pardon My Past* in which Fred MacMurray was playing a dual role for some illicit purpose. Well, it came to town in the same week as Tex Morton's rodeo — or 'Buck-jumping Show' as it was called — which I also needed passionately to attend. My parents were opposed to the latter entertainment; my grandmother, living with us at the time, as grandparents so often did in those far-off days, said she'd shout me to the pictures on the Saturday if I'd only stop being so relentless about the buck-jumping. But I wouldn't. Somehow I finally got to see Tex and Sister Dorrie from whose mouth — in profile, I hasten to add — he shot cigarettes. As it turned out, not one of the equine stars would do its stuff ('Horses, like humans, have their off-nights', Tex tried), and then someone in the crowd yelled, 'Put the nigger on the horse', referring to Tex's off-sider. This produced from Tex the great reply: 'Jackie is not a nigger. He is a coloured boy.' I felt I was in the presence of the higher tolerance as we all applauded. Certainly it was the only high-spot in the last such entertainment I ever attended. It was a total washout — and I didn't get to see *Pardon My Past*, and still haven't. Some cruel injustice was at work there which I couldn't quite work out.

But what a lot of strange and fascinating information about Life one picked up from the movies. What I wondered was all the fuss about in a Paramount comedy, *Standing Room Only*, in which Fred MacMurray as a businessman of some kind and Paulette Goddard as his (famously fetching) secretary could only find one room in which to sleep in wartime Washington? I mean, there were two beds in the room as I recall, but it seemed that more was at issue than just space. Again, in a no doubt deservedly forgotten romantic comedy called *She Went to the Races*, I remember being nonplussed by Ava Gardner's attempts to be friendly towards (i.e., seduce) the hero (James Craig) by offering disgusting drinks. Cocktails, they were, with never a suggestion of a nice glass of lemonade or any of the other liquors I was partial to. It made me wonder what adults were up to. And the way she was dressed for a simple meal at home. So unlike our own domestic life. More significantly, I was often much struck with the effortless way the male protagonists would think of clever, witty things to say to the women they were setting out to impress. William Holden, bemoaning the lot of undervalued screenwriters, might have had me in mind when he remarked sardonically in *Sunset Boulevard* that 'audiences don't know somebody sits down and writes a picture; they think the actors make it up as they go along.' I never thought of screenwriters doing the spade work for those suave types. It didn't seem to me it could be that easy to come up with such repartee, and, as I moved along into adolescence, I found it actually wasn't so. But I tried. The movies never stopped having their beneficial effects on me.

There was more going on in life than the movies of course, but hardly any of it was comparably absorbing. For a brief period stamp-collecting was a secondary obsession and so, a little later, was tennis, which for a few years was of life-and-death importance to me. Saturday mornings would be spent anxiously scanning the skies. What did I care whether or not we were in the grip of a drought? Certainly not at all if it interfered with my pleasures. And the passion for reading never slackened. Looking back, and indeed forward, I think there was always something obsessive in the way I went about either study or hobbies. As for study, I was always coming unpopularly top in exams; in the subjects I didn't understand, such as physics or the meteorological aspects of geography, I simply learnt the teachers' notes by heart and gave them back at exam time. They were in no position to disagree with what I'd written since it was word-for-word what they'd dictated. To this day, I can almost recite Ampère's Swimming Law ('Suppose a man is swimming in the direction of the current...'), and you'd scarcely credit how useful this has been to me. I was persuaded to do Physics and Chemistry and Maths at Year 11, so that, Don Hewitt, the only other boy at this level and still my friend, could be persuaded to stay at Nhill. Now I just write obsessively, but the seeds were being sown in those early reviews of films seen and unseen, and my annual scholarly summations of the year in film. This latter of course required some inventiveness in filling the gaps that were no fault of mine.

Chapter Three
City lights

The one unequivocally great thing about leaving home to study at the University of Melbourne was that I was now free to go to as many films as I liked — and I did. I had done sufficiently well in my Matriculation exams to be awarded a Secondary Teachers' Studentship, which would pay me enough money to live on, and which would then be entitled to 'bond' me for three years' teaching when I graduated. I'd also done well enough to be accepted into the First Year Honours course in English and French. I remember vividly sitting with my parents in the office of the Principal of the Secondary Teachers' College, Miss Alice Hoy, who was interviewing us about my prospective course. 'Do I take it, Mr McFarlane, that you have an Honours course in mind?' she asked. My father thought she was speaking to him and his startled face registered only 'Search me.' Certainly I'd never been addressed as Mr McFarlane before, perhaps not surprising in one who was only sixteen and would remain so until 31 May of that year, the last possible date for turning seventeen so as to obtain special dispensation for admission. This meant that I was the youngest, or equal youngest, student at the university.

If this makes me sound like a youthful prodigy, nothing in the ensuing four years would substantiate such an image. From having been a maniacally conscientious high-school student, when I wasn't being maniacal about the movies and those other interests such as philately and tennis, I quickly adjusted to the pleasures of having no one telling me what to do. Consequently, what followed was a deeply undistinguished First Year Honours course, a result offset by the fact that I did see 104 films in that year. To my very great credit, I missed only one lecture to do so, and that was for *Pagan Love Song*, never guessing, at the time, at aquastar Esther Williams's raunchy history (see her recent autobiography, *The Million Dollar Mermaid*, 2000, in which she lets it all hang out — and a very repulsive spectacle it makes). I was just conscientious enough in first year to go to lectures and tutorials, but not enough to make any serious use of them.

For one thing, I was about two years younger (and more naïve) than anyone else in the daunting tutorials, in which my strategy was to sit in the middle of a semi-circle of students, so that when we were questioned in turn about what we'd made of, say, 'The Waste Land', I would murmur, 'I can only agree with what Miss Moon or Mr Stowell has said,' and hope the tutor would pass on. For another thing, though, I do think that what was offered in first year English was unlikely to inspire one whose favoured reading at the time was the likes of A.J. Cronin or John Steinbeck. For instance, take *Pamela* or *Humphrey Clinker* and the whole batch of fat eighteenth-century novels, followed by the unspeakable George Borrow, or the arcane reaches of Hopkins, Yeats and Eliot. I came to appreciate these latter three in time, but never felt the slightest interest in going back to those eighteenth-century chaps, until 2006, when I finally read Sterne's *Tristram Shandy* as part of the research for a book about the director, Michael Winterbottom, who made a playful film version of it as *A Cock and Bull Story*. Having wrestled with Sterne's *A Sentimental Journey* at age sixteen, I'd decided, as a special treat to myself, never to read another word of his. If you hung on bravely during first year, you'd be rewarded by Samuel Butler's *The Way of All Flesh*, though I was too young and ignorant to understand what it was so wittily satirising, *Anna Karenina* and *A Passage to India* in third term, to all of which I have since returned with huge satisfaction. As for first year Honours French, at which I'd thought (erroneously as it happened) I might be rather proficient, Dr R.T. Sussex warned that we'd be failed if he even suspected us of reading *Madame Bovary* or *Le Rouge et le Noir* in translation. I was suitably cowed by this threat but the pleasure quotient remained dispiritingly low, and I've ever since thought the French should stick to cooking and the occasional film, such as Max Ophuls' *La Ronde* which, in 1952, I thought was about as sexy as film could be. Renoir, the *nouvelle vague* and many a later director have made me aware that they could be as good at movies as at *pâtisseries* but I've remained largely resistant to French literature.

The eighteenth century was not a patch on the easy pleasures of the Melbourne movie scene. Now, I was well-placed, except financially, to see not only new films as they opened at city cinemas, but also revivals of famous films I'd either been too young to see or over which I'd lost the battle with my parents. There were sixteen cinemas in the city proper (not counting the several newsreel theatrettes), and dozens more in the suburbs. The city cinemas were of course more luxurious than anything I had been used to; it is hard to imagine how they could have been less so. The most lavish in Melbourne were probably the State (of Moorish inspiration, and with a starlit ceiling; it is now mostly used for revival meetings) and the Regent (now used for staging musical comedies, such as *Priscilla, Queen of the Desert*), though the Capitol in Swanston Street, with its Walter Burley Griffin ceiling so cunningly lit, was no doubt architecturally superior. My friends and I were of course routinely to be found in the cheapest seats, at least till the lights went down, but it was different when you were taking a girl. Then, if you wanted to be impressive, it was Dress Circle or nothing, not to speak of chocolates and drinks at interval. You were ruined financially after one of these nights.

But the films! Among the dozens of revivals, I at last saw *Gone With the Wind* (at the Palais, St Kilda), *The Private Life of Henry VIII* (at the Plaza, with Merle Oberon as Anne Boleyn asking poignantly, 'Will my hair sit straight when my head falls?'), *The Hunchback of Notre Dame* (at the Plaza, Essendon), the Marx brothers in *At the Circus* (at the St James, later Metro, Bourke Street), David Lean's definitive *Great Expectations* (at the Savoy, Russell Street), the all-time cult favourite *Casablanca* (at the Australia Cinema, Collins Street), *Key Largo* (at the Esquire, Bourke Street, with Bogart and Bacall doing *noir* things), the seminal

Western *Stagecoach* (a university screening, with John Wayne riding shotgun, Thomas Mitchell as cultivated boozing doctor, and Claire Trevor, archetypal golden-hearted trollop, a type now much missed), *Brief Encounter* (at the Grosvenor, and still perhaps the most poignant screen love story) and many other 'reissues' or 'revivals' as they were called at the Regal Essendon, near where I was boarding, or in remote suburbs like Preston and Burnley. (The very names of the cinemas, or 'theatres' as they were apt to be called then, carry a nostalgic charge for me, and perhaps for others of comparable vintage.) I was filling in crucial gaps in my film-going experience and this was far more attractive to me than getting on with critical reading about *Pamela* or *Humphrey Clinker*. Nothing was too out of the way in so good a cause.

Only my Essendon landlady, the kind mother of a former Nhill teacher, would utter reproving remarks about my apparent light-mindedness in relation to my course and try to direct me to higher things. I listened very politely to this; then went on my light-minded way. She also said she thought my parents would be very disappointed to find that I'd taken up smoking. This happened one Saturday night at the end of my second year, when I was sitting bored in my Essendon room, not getting on with the study I so desperately needed for the exam on the following Monday. I suddenly decided to try smoking, never having had so much as a surreptitious puff down in the school bike-shed as you were meant to. I went out, bought a packet of ten Black-and-Whites, then conscientiously smoked one every half-hour, deciding that cigarettes and I were made for each other. Fifty years on, I long for the morning in which the newspapers tell us that 'recent university studies' have found smoking to be good for us after all. Friends with medical training assure me that this is not likely. I left the house where I boarded in Essendon to spend my last two university years living at an inner-city Education Department hostel. It was adjacent to a brothel, it was claimed, though I didn't know anyone who'd actually researched the matter, was within walking distance of city cinemas, and there was absolutely no one to speculate on whether or not I was using my time wisely. Looking back, I think I was really being unusually far-sighted for one so young.

It wasn't just a matter of seeing 104 films that came between me and those higher things, like my course; I was also slavishly committing my thoughts on film to paper. Only an exercise book, actually, but, as time went on, my university career (how inaccurately business-like that sounds) extended my chances to write about films and plays. In my second year, to be truthful, I began to enjoy my English Honours course, when the nineteenth century dominated, with Jane Austen, Thomas Hardy, Henry James and Matthew Arnold, to whose melancholy I felt very attuned, though who knows why, since I had nothing whatever to be melancholy about. Youthful romanticism, I expect. In this second year, writing about film took another turn. I co-edited with Gordon Kirby, then-theatre critic for the student paper, *Farrago*, and a legendary figure round the university, a slim journal called *Film Bulletin*, which appeared under the auspices of the University Film Society. Kirby was invariably busy, whether as theatre editor or producing plays and occasionally even at the State Library, his place of paid employment. As a result, *Film Bulletin* was largely written, typed (with two fingers, on *Farrago* office type-writers, with more or less the approval of the editor, friend Gavan Daws, who had actually persuaded me to miss the lecture in favour of *Pagan Love Song* the previous year), photocopied (by whatever was the process of the day — Gestetner possibly?) and relentlessly sold (for sixpence) by me, at the Union building's doorway or in tutorials, wherever two or three were gathered together. I suppose friends felt they could hardly refuse — it was only sixpence, after all — but I also pestered tutors and lecturers I knew, and, considering the cost, they probably felt it would be mean to say no. Gordon would be nagged by me into providing his copy, the editorial and information about European films, while I wrote almost all the reviews, full of severe judgments, like that which proclaimed *Singin' in the Rain* a sad disappointment after *An American in Paris*, or that

The Cruel Sea 'falls down in many places', with directors only just getting noticed in those pre-*auteurist* days, while the actors commanded most space.

Actually, I did take the reviewing business seriously, and was aware that for the first time I was writing for an audience beyond myself. We'd rashly said the journal would appear fortnightly; when I add that four issues appeared in three years, our folly will be apparent. One idiosyncrasy of this publication occurred in the listing of recommended viewing, including reissues. Instead of putting the stars' names in brackets after the title, I would indulge my delight in character actors, so that *The Father of the Bride* had '(Billie Burke, Moroni Olsen)' listed with never a reference to Spencer Tracy or Elizabeth Taylor, or a revival of *The Man in Grey* which named Raymond Lovell and Martita Hunt, by-passing Margaret Lockwood and James Mason, or by putting in the star's name as an afterthought, as in the case of Guinness (wrongly spelt) after four of his supporting players in *The Man in the White Suit*. I only stopped this process when a friend told me she thought I must be referring to a different film, and that what I was doing was very misleading. But quirks like this and some deeply ridiculous opinions to one side, *Film Bulletin* was still important to me: it confirmed what I'd first supposed about age ten: that what I really wanted to do was to *write about* films, rather than, more creatively, *make* them, and I've done so compulsively for more than fifty further years. The university also offered the pleasure of *talking* about films — especially to the wildly knowledgeable Kirby and the astringent Daws, who loved musicals and abhorred sentimentality, disdaining *Random Harvest* which I decades later wrote about as an almost perfect romantic melodrama, John Fox, with whom I'd have a forty-year conversation about films, and others, like the marvellously good-natured Rhyll Jones (now Rhyll Nance), who were interested if less well informed — and less obsessive. And there was another Wimmera lad, Graeme Coulson, who was happy to be bullied into seeing a great many films (e.g., a double-bill revival of *Key Largo* and *Nobody Runs Forever*, with John

Garfield and the gorgeous Geraldine Fitzgerald) he wouldn't have thought of, and in a reverse action persuaded me to join the Lacrosse Club, at which he excelled and at which I predictably didn't. But I wasn't greatly drawn to the more solemn discussions I sometimes had with members of the Film Society: I was still too desperately catching up with the mainstream and trying to plug gaps in the feature-film world to have much time left for earnest documentaries and experimental film, and I'm sure the loss was mine.

My university years were interrupted by National Service, at the end of my second year, another ill-effect of having gone to the university at sixteen, as my friends had all done their 'nasho' at the end of first year. In my brief but exciting military career, I managed with no difficulty to stay a private for the whole time. I like to think that this was because I'd decided to 'stay with the men' rather than accept promotion to the heady heights of lance-corporal, but truth compels me to admit that such advancement was never offered to me. The fact that I'd once, on rifle-range practice, nearly shot the platoon commander possibly contributed to this oversight on the part of the army. This came about as a result of my pulling the trigger instead of, as instructed, putting on the safety-catch — a mistake anyone might have made — while he went forward to inspect the targets. Also, while we were supposedly doing 'picket duty' by night, to make sure communists weren't infiltrating Puckapunyal while the soldiery slept, it was common practice to sit in the comparative comfort of the company office and read all the confidential records relating to those in 'C' Company. About me, I found the following summary: 'Quiet but good type. Appears more interested in his private life than in the army'. How could they have guessed this? Again, as in tutorials, I made a point of always being in the middle of the ranks for marching, so as to be unnoticed if out of step. Or for exercises such as dismantling and reassembling a Bren gun (so useful as this has been to me in later life): the more times I watched others engaged in such intricacies, the more chance I had of sliding through without attracting the sergeant's heavy wit.

Anyway, for one brief shining moment, I became the hero of the hour by getting our entire company out of a night parade. I drew the attention of Warrant-Officer Kinrade in charge of this manoeuvre (protecting a few gum trees from an overnight raid by our country's enemies) as we marched past the Puckapunyal hall to the fact that *This Happy Breed* was screening that evening. 'Really, sir, it's a very patriotic film, about what we're actually learning to fight for here,' I confided to him. He (the near-victim of my little error in the rifle range) was much moved by this lie, and the entire company was marched not out on to the surrounding desolate hills but into the hall to watch Celia Johnson, John Mills and others stiffen our resolve never to let down Her Majesty and the 15th National Service Training Battalion. Other films I recall seeing there were *Something to Live For*, a triangular romance about recovering alcoholics, and — could anything have been less likely to succeed here? — the screen version of *The Glass Menagerie*, starring Gertrude Lawrence, not really a name for the troops to conjure with. The only other film-related aspect of this three-month period of learning how to keep the nation strong was that my mother regularly sent on my copies of *Picturegoer* in boxes of cakes, and the other occupants of the hut seized upon pictures of Marilyn Monroe and other assorted lovelies as they grabbed slices of passion-fruit shortbread.

On return from serving my country, I took the easy way out, dropped out of my Honours course and decided to finish with a Pass degree that year. I had only seven contact hours per week and found myself averaging perhaps four, so exigent were the other claims on my time. For one thing, I became theatre editor of *Farrago*. While in Puckapunyal, I'd noticed in the *Age* the photo of a very pretty girl I'd known a little at the university the year before. She and a number of other hopefuls were expressing their enthusiasm about the start of the academic year and I felt strongly that I'd like to take her out when I returned to civilian life. Well, Kirby, the then-theatre editor, offered me two free seats, so that I could take this girl, Monica Wood, who later became Monica Maughan, the well-known Melbourne actress, to the Commencement Play, *Romeo and Juliet*, in return for writing a long review of it. I never for a moment considered letting lack of qualifications stand in my way; I *needed* those tickets and was strapped for cash, having unwisely spent most of my National Service pay as I got it, and the rest had gone on a dinner-suit to equip me for a prospectively dazzling social life. Some time later that year, I replaced Kirby as *Farrago's* theatre critic (with his acquiescence, not as an aspiring take-over), and used this position to offer solemn film reviews as well. If free seats constituted one of the perks of reviewing, another advantage — at least I thought it would be — was that it might be a way of impressing young women otherwise immune to my charms. 'I'm reviewing this play/film for *Farrago*. Would you like to come?' I would say with, I hoped, a persuasive worldly noncha-lance. It is galling to recall, but my handshake and brief exchange of nullities with the Duke of Edinburgh in 1954 was actually more effective with those I wanted to impress. He came briefly to the university during the famous post-war Royal Visit and met with members of the SRC (Student Representative Council) to which, for some ambitious reason I can't now recall, I'd been elected.

In this dubious editorial capacity, I wrote what I now think must have been an impudent letter to Dame Sybil Thorndike and Sir Lewis Casson, in Melbourne for poetry recitals, asking if they would agree to be interviewed for *Farrago*. To my astonishment I got a handwritten letter back from her saying, 'Yes, of course I will give you an interview, do ring me'. So I interviewed them in Iona Avenue, Toorak, where her son John lived. She did most of the talking, partly because Lewis was more than a bit deaf. She would sometimes turn to him and repeat more loudly those penetrating questions and views I'd just uttered. She had an immense warmth and vitality, justly celebrated in Jonathan Croall's wonderful 2008 biography, with its subtitle, *A Star of Life*; and she had that way that some people have, as decades later I found in Richard Attenborough, of making you think that nothing is more crucial in their lives than talking to you at that moment. She seemed an extraordinarily good woman, who

IN AN INTERVIEW WITH FARRAGO:

Cassons advise student actors

By Farrago Theatre Editor
BRIAN McFARLANE

TO call the thirty-five minutes I spent with the Cassons an interview fails to give the correct impression of what actually happened.

A better way of describing it is to say that for most of the time I listened fascinated to the impressions of two of today's greatest theatrical figures on plays, films, and players.

The rest of the time was spent in answering Dame Sybil's own questions about our University drama, which interests her tremendously.

In the course of the discussion, both Dame Sybil and Sir Lewis gave some very sound advice to student actors and student drama.

"Tell them not to get too stuck on themselves," said Dame Sybil.

She stressed the need for humility and the need to act for love of the theatre rather than love of exhibitionism.

"Be humble and work hard" seemed to her the best counsel she could offer to young players.

Dame Sybil cited the case of Gladys Cooper, "who could have just sat back and looked beautiful but, instead, worked hard and became a fine actress."

Slickness bad

Sir Lewis warned amateurs against aiming at slickness rather than at adherence to the author's aim.

"It's better to drive home each point made by the author than to see how many ideas you can throw at the audience per minute.

"This way some will arrive home, but many will just drop by the wayside."

Both were particularly interested to hear whether our dramatic clubs attempted many Australian plays.

Fortunately I could mention "Fire on the Snow" as well as "Ned Kelly," about which silence is probably kinder.

They recommended trying plays not likely to come up against competition from the commercial theatre.

New play-wright

Sir Lewis recommended particularly the plays of new playwright John Whiting ("Marching Song," "The Saint's Day," and "Penny for a Song," — "very clever and very difficult").

I asked Dame Sybil about her attitude to film-making (we have seen her in "Britannia Mews," "Melba," "Stagefright" and many others).

She finds the experience very enjoyable though the lack of continuity and audience response, all-important to a stage-player, keep films for her at the level of an "interesting technical experiment."

Her last film, "The Weak and the Wicked," a prison story, she thoroughly enjoyed making, because she appears in the film's only comic episode and because she plays with Athene Leyler, her greatest friend.

Among the people we spoke of were Gladys Cooper, Athene Leyler ("so amusing"), Jill Esmond ("a most thoughtful actress"), Laurence Olivier and Vivien Leigh, for whom Dame Sybil has tremendous admiration ("such vitality and glamour," her alway "Cleopatra"— wonderful!"), Marie Lohr and Wendy Hiller, who worked with Dame Sybil in "Waters of the Moon."

It sounded like a Who's Who of the British theatre by one who knows them and has worked with them.

Invigorating hour

To talk with the Cassons is an invigorating and stimulating experience.

Their knowledge and love of the theatre is only a part of their charm — the rest is the sincerity and warmth of their interest in the world in general, the world outside their own particular milieu.

SIR LEWIS CASSON AND DAME SYBIL THORNDIKE.
—Block by courtesy of "The Age."

Farrago, *7 September 1954*

would regard it as important to set a very green young man (from 'Greenland' indeed, like Oliver Twist) at his ease. A couple of nights later, I went to the Cassons' poetry recital at the Assembly Hall, which was an exhilarating experience. Lewis forgot his lines a bit, so she sat him down and gave him a glass of water, and we all applauded. I was trying to impress Joan, a brand-new girl-friend, and we went back-stage afterwards as the great lady had invited me to do. There was quite a crowd of people there, but, when she saw me, she waved and said, 'How nice to see you again,' and turned to Joan and boomed, 'Oh, we had such a stimulating chat the other day. He was so challenging.' Not so, of course, but who cared about that? It did my ego, and, in Joan's eyes, what my father would have called 'a power of good'. Amateurish as my interviewing technique no doubt was, the occasion must have started something that would come to fruition in the 1990s in two books wholly given over to interviews with people I'd admired in British cinema, but more of that later.

Mention of the Cassons recalls another peripheral pleasure of my university years: the possibility of seeing, in the (sometimes age-ing) flesh, film stars imported to give (sometimes delusive) box-office potency to plays at the city theatres — the Comedy, the Princess, Her Majesty's and the Tivoli. It's worth noting that students could then afford to go to the commercial theatre, and I saw virtually everything. The Cassons, though elderly, were still major names in British theatre, and in the year after their poetry recitals they joined another major name, Ralph Richardson, and his wife Meriel Forbes, to present two plays by Terence Rattigan at the Princess, *Separate Tables* and *The Sleeping Prince*. There was no doubt of their pulling power, but in the years just before this it had to be admitted that Jessie Matthews (in *Larger than Life*), Evelyn Laye and Frank Lawton (in *September Tide*) were past their days of glory. Matthews, in particular, had been one of the top two or three film stars of 1930s Britain, but by the early 50s her lustre was tarnished. As for poor drunken Diana Barrymore, on hand to *Light Up the Sky*, a lesser Moss Hart vehicle, it is arguable that she never had a day of glory, but I remembered her fondly in *Eagle Squad-ron*, one of those Hollywood war films set in a Britain that owed more to California than to the Home Counties. And she was the first film star I ever spoke to. *Farrago* editor Gavan Daws and I were members of a matinee audience of twenty-five at the Princess, towards the end of 1951, and we'd rather enjoyed her and went backstage to tell her so, partly to offset the ignominy of being part of that meagre audience some of whose members threw coins at her. Much classier, of course, were Anthony Quayle and Diana Wynyard in touring productions of the Shakespeare Memorial Theatre, Stratford. Wynyard, who made only rare but notable film appearances (as Lady Chiltern, for instance, in *An Ideal Husband*), was an actress of rare subtlety and a discreet ladylike sexiness, and she died sadly young in 1964. And who, I wonder, remembers Jimmy Hanley, prole leading man in such British films as *The Way Ahead* and the 'Huggett' series, who starred at the Tivoli in *To Dorothy a Son* in 1952? His children by Dinah Sheridan, Jenny and (Sir) Jeremy Hanley, fifty years later came to a book launch of mine in London, Jeremy looking for all the world like his very likable father. The fact that I'd seen them in films gave these players for me a special cachet unlikely to be shared by local *actors*, who no doubt saw them as taking the bread from their mouths.

It's no wonder I hadn't a lot of time to spare for my studies. Not only was I going to films at a rate my allowance could hardly keep up with, I was then confiding my impressions to my notebooks or exchanging them with more or less like-minded friends. In the 1950s, film had not yet become a respectable academic pursuit and many would have thought my preoccupation with it indicative of a trivial mind. As well as viewing and writing about films, I was always reading about them. I remained loyal to *Picture Show* and *Picturegoer* until, despite efforts to jazz up their pages with pop singers and 'gifts as worn by the stars', both folded at the end of the 1950s. But, and not a moment too soon, my tastes were maturing and I began to read the British Film Institute's quarterly journal, *Sight and Sound*, which was a much more serious affair than any reading about film I'd come across before. In its high-minded way, it focused often on foreign-language films. Only very select Hollywood or British films found their way into its review pages. Famous names — and names that would become famous — were to be found writing thoughtful pieces on matters more serious than my earlier reading had had in mind. We were offered, say, John Grierson on fellow documentarist Robert Flaherty, reprints of articles by Aldous Huxley and Thomas Mann on the art of the cinema, and 'Personal Notes' by Jean Renoir. Among those of whom more would be heard as filmmakers, Lindsay Anderson and Karel Reisz were regular reviewers, and in Anderson's reviews of John Ford's films — *The Quiet Man* and *The Sun Shines Bright* — I began to understand my own veneration for the irascible Irish-American director. It was here that I began to learn about 'foreign' cinema giants such as Eisenstein (in pieces by Marie Seton and director Thorold Dickinson) and Luis Buñuel (appraised by director-to-be Tony Richardson), coinciding for me with my first exposure to non-anglophone films at what then passed for art-houses in Melbourne. We all went to the Savoy to see the Swedish film *One Summer of Happiness,* for art of course, not for its notorious lakeside nude love scene. In the mid-fifties, when I had a bit more cash to spare, another British journal called *Films and Filming* also appeared, on a monthly basis. Though some of the same writers appeared in it and in *Sight and Sound,* the new journal was negotiating a middle way between the austerities of the older one and the easier diets of the declining fan magazines, and it lasted for thirty years. I was happy to read *anything* about film, even the wrappers around 'Fantales': each of these chocolate-coated toffees (specially designed to pull out your dental fillings) was reached only after reading a couple of mini-biographies of the stars.

Whatever else I was up to during those four years at the University of Melbourne, the one continuing activity was the writing about films. In 1951, off the parental hook for the first time and seeing all those films, I also wrote short reviews of many of them, so that, looking at them now, I wonder that I managed to scrape through my course even at the ignominious level that I did. In each of the succeeding years, while also writing for *Film Bulletin* and, in 1953 and 1954, for *Farrago,* I was reviewing everything else as well, filling Embassy Reporters Note Books and the like with my sage pronouncements on the films I saw, as well as a yearly round-up at the end of 52, 53 and 54. It has not been good for my ego to re-read these documents after fifty years: their style was, I should think, pretty much influenced by *Picturegoer* or the local reviewers in the *Listener-In* or the *Argus.* That is, they engage in more story-telling than anyone can have wanted, and I was for most of these outpourings the sole reader, with some comments about the acting, always highlighting supporting players who often gave 'sound/amusing character studies', especially in British films. I often found performances 'deeply moving', like Olivia De Havilland's in *Gone with the Wind,* and, unsurprisingly, Merle Oberon was 'genuinely moving as Anne Boleyn' in *The Private Life of Henry VIII.* How could you be 'falsely moving'? Certainly, though, in 2008 Natalie Portman was not even shallowly moving as ill-fated Anne in *The Other Boleyn Girl.* The

British war film, *They Were Not Divided*, was 'deeply moving', and so was that very capable actor Laurence Olivier in *Carrie*. Various recurring phrases such as 'on the distaff side' and 'delicious satire' suggest someone not yet sure of his own style — and not yet under the sway of the loftier aspirations of *Sight and Sound*, which I began subscribing to in 1953, and still do. Another phrase whose cadences I liked without being too sure of its implied distinctions was that relating to a woman who 'loved not wisely but too well'. There was a lot of that sort of thing about in those days, in films such as *My Foolish Heart*, its capricious organ belonging to Susan Hayward.

As I re-read these callow pieces, I am shocked at how forceful and opinionated they are. For example, of *The Dancing Years*, a musical adapted from Ivor Novello, 'The story is extremely hackneyed and feeble, the photography is not always good — Giselle Préville in particular is often badly photographed — and the dialogue is decidedly corny'. And I summed up *Where No Vultures Fly* with a warning that I hope Ealing Studios took to its heart: '… the makers haven't realised that it takes more than sincerity to make an entertaining film. Scenic effects are all very well in their way, but, more than these, a film needs a sense of drama, and that is what is missing here'. There is too sometimes an Olympian tone, as in the opening sentence of a review of *Waterfront*, an unpretentious British second feature, an early film of Richard Burton's: 'This is the sort of film I like to praise. There is a forthright honesty in the telling of the story… Yet it somehow fails to be really moving', or in this portentous start on *Storm Warning*: 'Every once in a while Hollywood sends us a film uncompromising in its adultness and realism' and the review finishes boldly with 'This is an outstanding film'. There was also a tendency to address myself fearlessly to a non-existent readership. My review of *He Ran All the Way* begins: 'Make no mistake about this. Shelley Winters is an actress of the first order. This fact is driven home forcefully in this grim but gripping drama. Shorn of every vestige of glamour, she turns in a completely realistic and very moving character study'. I wonder whom I imagined I was addressing when I ended my account of Cecil B DeMille's *The Greatest Show on Earth* with: 'Memo:

watch the Grahame girl [Gloria, that was]. She's potential star material if ever there was'.

I was very big on 'realism' which I identified at work in the reissue of two early David Lean films, *This Happy Breed* and *Brief Encounter* ('No film I remember ever came so close to life', I wrote in my note-pad), as well as in American 'social conscience' films such as Cy Endfield's *Sound of Fury*, a 'strong indictment against mob rule', or Elia Kazan's *On the Waterfront*, which 'makes no concession to Hollywood compromise, thereby ringing the bell of truth'. The latter, I was pleased to add, 'reminds us that Hollywood can still startle us by rising above its self-imposed standards of mediocrity'. In fact, with the coming to prominence of actors such as Marlon Brando and directors like Kazan and Fred Zinnemann, Hollywood actually *was* entering on a major period of achievement in the realist mode. But no one was theorising then about what was meant by 'realism'. It just vaguely implied some sort of correspondence with what one took to be comparable events, circumstances and people, in the 'real world'. Similarly no one, with the possible exception of the British journal *Sequence*, which I didn't see until the 1980s, long after it had ceased publication, was analysing notions of genre. So, loving Westerns as I did, I would try to find more in, say, *The Gunfighter*, *High Noon* or *Shane* than 'mere' action — I'd grown out of that — and was praising them for offering more 'realistic' pictures of life out West. How could I possibly have known? But, again, there was no one, in relation to either film or my more respectable discipline, literature, to make me think about realism as a mode of representation, rather than as a critical criterion. (As for *High Noon*, 'Not since *Stagecoach*', your reviewer considered, 'has there been such a deeply exciting treatment of a Western theme'. This kind of lofty opinion is sprinkled throughout the surviving notepads, and I think it is very brave of me to quote them here.)

In all my time at the university, such a preoccupation with the movies was essentially a guilty pleasure. It was acceptable to have gone to Continental films at the old Savoy in Russell Street or the Australia

Cinema in Collins Street. As a bonus, these films were also much sexier than mainstream fare, but that of course was not why any of us went to, say, *The Sinner,* starring the very sensual Hildegard Neff, let alone the aforementioned Swedish *One Summer of Happiness,* with its tasteful nudity. (As to the latter, was Ulla Jacobsson's the first bare breast to be seen on a respectable Melbourne screen? It was certainly the first I ever saw.) Merely to have put oneself through the reading of subtitles was to have acquired serious cultural capital. Going to 'a good British film' was next in the aesthetic hierarchy, while Hollywood was nowhere as far as prestige was concerned — was, in fact, used as a pejorative adjective. The serious study of Hollywood was still a decade or so away. I certainly took it seriously, though not in the theorised way scholars of later decades would. My 1954 round-up was very severe about the potentialities of CinemaScope which had reached Melbourne that year, via epics such as *The Robe,* and the travelogue vacuities of *Three Coins in the Fountain.* From the nineteen productions in the new process, I excepted from general obloquy only Nunnally Johnson's Cold War thriller, *Night People,* starring Gregory Peck. A current girlfriend called Pam said she wanted to see this, and, though I normally did the choosing, I let her have her way on this occasion, and not only did it boast (according to my *Farrago* review) 'a punchy plot, intelligent dialogue and a cast of distinguished players', but one of the latter proved to be none other than Jill Esmond, who had so changed my life years before in *My Pal Wolf.*

For the rest of these wide-screen wonders, I wrote challengingly that they were marked by 'a pretentious vulgarity of approach quite unwarranted by a footling, empty narrative, a lack of anything approaching incisive character-drawing, and, in the matter of stars, an emphasis on physical rather than histrionic assets', I mean, how high-minded can you be at nineteen? CinemaScope (and other wide-screen systems) became in short order a fact of life as the decade unfolded, but though I, like everyone else grew accustomed to it, and of course it proved not to be, of itself, inimical to more intimate, humanely-oriented filmmaking, to this day I remain suspicious of films which parade their size and cost. As recently as 2005, I wrote a critical article for Melbourne's *Metro*, with the title, 'Size Doesn't Matter: Big Stupid Films', in which I vented some of the sort of spleen I was dealing to the 1950s CinemaScope epics. Back then, the first films in the new system justified apprehensiveness about what might be the future of films whose chief interest was in the interplay of human relations. As theatre editor of *Farrago*, I gradually and insidiously inserted film reviews into the paper. One of the films I championed in the face of the growing elephantiasis as I saw it was John Ford's beautiful elegiac *The Sun Shines Bright*. I used such films, and reissues such as Garbo's *Marie Walewska*, as sticks with which to beat the new vulgarity I had diagnosed.

Somehow, and without distinction, I got through a B.A. and a Dip.Ed. by the end of 1954, and at the age of twenty, a bit older but not much wiser, I was about to venture into what the Education Department referred to as 'the field', a euphemism for remote schools in the far corners of Victoria. The teaching positions were announced to us all at a public assembly by Miss Hoy, who got a round of unintended and undeserved laughter when she said, in relation to these appointments, 'If any of the married men feel they have

Farrago, 29 June 1954

not received satisfaction, they should see me after this meeting.' I was unmarried and was not sure that my posting to Terang in the Western District of Victoria would, in any case, provide satisfaction. In all sorts of ways, I found that it did.

Chapter Four
Back to the bush

Writing more than fifty years later, I still have the vividest memory of my train journey from Melbourne to Terang on the day before the High School started on the first Tuesday in February 1955. Naturally I didn't want to arrive there a moment before it was necessary. As I said to myself, 'You've had a good life, Brian, and you couldn't have expected it to last forever.' After the glittering urban life of the last four years — well, that's how it seemed to me in retrospect as I sat in the Victorian 'red rattler' train on an overcast morning — the prospect of returning to a country town, which was no bigger than the one I'd grown up in, seemed bleak indeed. In my compartment was a very nice young woman with whom I fell into conversation, outlining some of my misgivings about what lay ahead. Next day I met her again — in my 6th form English class at the High School. Wherever you are now Helen Bell, who can only have been two or three years younger than I was, I pay tribute to your discretion: as far as I know, she never spread about the place my disaffected and melancholy apprehensions.

Having been at the University for four years, and therefore knowing one's way about with all the sophistication available to a twenty-year-old, it was initially galling (and being salutary in the long run is never much of a consolation for that) to be the newest of the new and youngest of the young. Further, the headmaster, Mr Sainsbury, had also had this position at Nhill, and introduced me to the Terang student body as a former pupil of his, making me seem even more callow than I was (which was quite hard to do). A bluff and cheerful man, who liked golf and a glass of beer, he proved a kind and forbearing principal, who would remind one only mildly that one was on yard duty and should cease playing Monopoly in the staffroom at lunch time and get out there to stop fights and organise rubbish collection. Later, when I was sharing a flat with another teacher, he would, with pretty well concealed exasperation, say, 'Brian and Johno, could you please take your smalls out of the boiler room before the inspectors get here tomorrow?' We habitually did our laundry in the Home Economics centre, for preference when there were no Domestic Science classes going on — this was certainly the preference of Marion Alexander (now Woods, and a friend to this day), who taught them — and hung our dripping clothes over the pipes in the boiler room to dry.

Actually, Mr Sainsbury's forbearance was even further tested when, at the end of the September holidays in 1955, I missed my train back to Terang, made a very feeble effort to hitch-hike, then rang to explain my situation. Or, rather, not so much to explain it as to divert attention from it. What had happened was this, though I did not confide it to Mr Sainsbury at this point. A pretty American film actress I liked, called Marsha Hunt, was appearing in Melbourne in the saucy (well, saucy for the 1950s) play, *The Little Hut*: I'd established only the most tangential contact — i.e., I went backstage to meet her — and had had the effrontery to invite her to coffee or a drink. No, coffee, I think; I wasn't sophisticated enough to carry off 'a drink'. Anyway, I was to collect her at her hairdresser's and off we'd go. She was an hour late, and it never occurred to me to say that I'd have to call it off because I had to catch a train back to Terang. We had coffee and she told me about working with William Powell, Laurence Olivier, Mickey Rooney, Claire Trevor and Greer Garson *et al*, as I watched the minutes slip past the time of my train's departure. When I phoned Mr Sainsbury, he bore up patiently, just telling me it was 'a bad business, Brian,' and all would have been more or less well if the *West Wimmera Mail*, learning of my assignation with the lovely Marsha, hadn't run a story with the bold heading: 'MARSHA HUNT TAKES TEA WITH NHILL TEACHER'. The fact that they'd given my home town rather than where I was teaching hardly helped matters. I was, as they used to say, sprung. But I recall Marsha Hunt with pleasure and admiration: she was one of those Hollywood players who stood up to the vile Senator McCarthy in the early 50s, risking her career in doing so.

But that is to skip a bit. You *can* be lucky. I really did think significant life was over when I was posted to the country. However, this most happily proved not to be the case, and, daunting mixture of naivety and intolerance that I was, I had the very great good fortune to fall in with some of the most entirely cultivated as well as endlessly kind people I have ever come across, before or since. To single out just one of them, I still think Mollie Bennett, wife of the Anglican vicar (he an imposing and eccentric figure), was the best cook and had the most genuinely sophisticated mind and sharpest wit I've ever come across — in the one person, at least. I remember being away one weekend when a teacher called Reg had brought his girlfriend down to Terang. On my return I asked Mollie, 'What was Reg's girlfriend like?' She replied: 'Oh, I think Reg can do better than that — and I'm sure she intends to.' Because these people were older than I (it was hard to be younger and still an adult), most have now gone to their just rewards. They tactfully encouraged me in the business of really growing up and supported a venture I initiated there and which gave me — and, I guess, them — so much pleasure. In the pre-television days of the mid-1950s, there was not a great deal of organised entertainment to be had in a small town, apart from the movies twice a week at the Mechanics Institute. A Melbourne friend with whom I was discussing this (i.e., complaining), said, 'Why don't you start a play-reading group?' By this time I'd left the house where I'd been boarding — a house and garden so tidy that, on my first night there before unpacking an ashtray, I'd been forced to dig a neat hole in the garden to bury my cigarette butts — and was now sharing the flat mentioned earlier. So, I put a notice in the local paper, the *Terang Express*, announcing a meeting to form the Terang Dramatic Society to be held at 8 Warrnambool Road for the following Tuesday. My flatmate and friend of more than fifty years, Johno Johnson, cooperative if less enthusiastic, and I for the next three years, on a fortnightly basis, tidied this apartment enough to ward off revulsion among numbers ranging from thirty to sixty-odd, sitting on beds, the floor, the folding-stools that they learned to bring, while they listened to readings of everything from Noël Coward to *Summer of the 17th Doll.*

The plays the group read were often the result of my knowing the films based on them, rather than having seen them performed. So, we started with *The Winslow Boy,* followed this with such titles as *Rebecca, The Women, Great Day, Blithe Spirit, The Man Who Came to Dinner, The Admirable Crichton, The Hasty Heart, The Browning Version, An Inspector Calls, Pygmalion, The Corn is Green, The Little Foxes* and so on. That is, essentially solid matinee fare: to establish the group, and it eventually had well over 100 members, we weren't going to risk, say, Jacobean tragedy or T.S. Eliot's doomed attempts to revive verse drama. All those titles listed were available for hire in readers' sets from the admirable Victorian Drama League, which is still a thriving concern as I write. As usual in such groups, there was a preponderance of women and this influenced the choice of plays, but it was still possible to field casts for such all-male enterprises as *Fire on the Snow, Journey's End, The Long and the Short and the Tall* and *The Caine Mutiny Court-Martial.* The Society got off to a very promising start perhaps partly because, in the mid-50s, television was still several years away from small country towns and people were glad of the diversion, of the sociability of it all, and of the degree of intellectual challenge it offered. They took the readings seriously enough for the results to be entertaining and/or stimulating for the listeners, in spite of the physical discomforts of 8 Warrnambool Road; discomforts that must have been increased by the high incidence of smoking, but no one would have thought of protesting about that in those far-off days. One man used to draw frowns as he tapped his 'Players' cigarette about ten times on the packet before lighting up; what could he have been hoping to achieve by this? One very old Welsh woman, mid 80s, had uncontested access to the single armchair, and sat smoking and coughing her way through the evening, her hair having gone quite yellow in front from the upward-curling results of her addiction. Johno grew quite tired of a very plump woman's flopping her considerable weight on his bed and gave her a shock one night by having built up some sturdy suitcases underneath it. She sat more decorously in future, and many took to bringing their own folding stools rather than sitting on sagging beds or the floor. Another woman used to cut out material on the floor in accordance with dress-making patterns, only pausing to trim her nails with her pinking shears. Such idiosyncrasies to one side, these gatherings were some of the most congenial and socially inclusive I've ever been involved in, drawing support from a wide social and intellectual range. All the readings were solemnly reviewed by me in the local press. Those who read these learnt to decode my last sentence which simply began 'The cast was completed by...' to mean that not all the readers were of uniformly high standard.

Big Crowd At Reading Of Popular Play

Sixty-two people eased their way into the meeting room at 8 Warrnambool Road, last Tuesday night, for Terang Dramatic Society's reading of Ray Lawlor's prize-winning Australian play, "Summer of the Seventeenth Doll."

RICH in characteristic humor, shot through with penetrating revelations of character and situation, the play depicts the seventeenth summer in which two Queensland cane-cutters, Roo and Barney, have come south to spend the "lay-off" season with two Melbourne barmaids in a Carlton terrace house.

The standard of reading was uniformly high. Ian Stuart and Daryl Rowley as the taciturn, defeated Roo and the likable womaniser, Barney, gave two excellent, vividly contrasted readings, and John Johnson was exactly in character as the young cane-cutter, Don, who has taken Roo's place as gang-leader.

Patricia King realised with great sympathy and sensitivity the emotionally adolescent Olive —this was a most admirable reading, full of vivid, authentic feeling, and Janet Teal as Pearl, determined to preserve her respectability at all costs, was touching and funny. Alison Bell as Bubba Ryan, the young girl next door who has idealized the "lay-off" season, read attractively and there was a delightful piece of comic characterisation from Kath Webb as Olive's dreadful old harridan of a mother.

The next reading will probably be "Anastasia," at the meeting on March 11.

Terang Express,
29 February 1958

However, we weren't going to be satisfied for long with merely *reading* plays, enjoyable as this was. *Performance*, on the stage of the Mechanics Institute, very quickly became our goal, and I, with virtually no qualifications for it, took on the role of director — or producer (as it used then to be called). After a one-act debut with Coward's *Fumed Oak*, a bitter comedy of a worm-who-turns husband confronting snivelling daughter, shrewish wife and malicious mother-in-law, we ventured into three acts the following year. Not once, but twice: first, with Esther McCracken's domestic comedy, *Quiet Weekend*, which the public so took to its bosom that we repeated it a month later, and, more ambitiously Coward's *This Happy Breed*, the film of which I had so movingly persuaded my national service warrant officer to let us see instead of doing a night manoeuvre. It was said that the performance of *This Happy Breed* led to tears in the stalls. Remember that this was before John Osborne's *Look Back in Anger* or Samuel Beckett's *Waiting for Godot* had made us wary of admiring or enjoying, say, Coward or Rattigan or Priestley. It became apparent that there were many people both gifted and enthusiastic and ready to participate on stage and back-stage — and that there was a gratifying audience for their work. The wife of one of the local doctors used to send her housekeeper, at 6 am on the day that bookings opened, down to the fruit shop where the box-office plans were held. The idea caught on and there would be a very encouraging queue snaking its way down the main street by the time I rode by on my bike to school at 8.45. In the following year, flushed with success, we elected to do two-night seasons which attracted 1100 patrons from a town whose population was barely 2000.

There was an immense amount of stimulating work done by a great many people who took to the business of being as professional as they could despite their amateur status, and various kinds of expertise were either tapped or emerged. By 'tapped' I mean for instance that Kelvin Brinsmead, the local electrician, fortunately for us a member of the Dramatic Society, undertook entirely the business of lighting, thereby minimising our chances of electrocution, while Dulcie Dow, who had her own hairdressing salon, was not a member but always turned up to help with hair and makeup, thereby ensuring that people would look like other people. Farmer Daryl Rowley devised a way of using large flattened Nescafé tins for securing the flats that made up the sets. The sets were painted in a cold and filthy shed behind the Mechanics Institute by Ila Grayland, an incredibly painstaking high-school colleague, who created templates for producing wallpaper effects on the sets of several plays. And the tenacious women who scoured the

Terang Mechanics Institute

town and outlying districts for appropriate items of stage décor became legendary as they homed in on the valuable *objets* of their friends' sitting-rooms. One woman claimed to have had her new gold brocade curtains fixed to the window frames so that they would be safe from the drama people. They weren't — and a handsome adornment they were to the set of *The Heiress* in 1960. Two other women became indispensable as stage manager and prompter respectively: they gave those on stage the sense of security they needed and were unflappably proficient about all they did.

Moving the CinemaScope screen to the back of the somewhat precariously raked stage for the erection of the set was always a tense business. It was on rollers, was heavy and unwieldy, and always threatened to career off into the auditorium, in defiance of the dozen or so of us trying to pull it on ropes to anchor it to the back of the stage. I remember a feeling of relief when my bank account (being earmarked for overseas travel) reached £300, which was what the screen was reputed to have cost. If worst came to worst, I thought heroically, I can replace it. What the outraged cinema patrons would have done to me if this disaster had occurred is best not to be thought of. Most memorably, in 1960, in connection with *The Heiress*, adapted from Henry James's *Washington Square*, we had the set up for dress rehearsal on the Sunday night, had to take it down and restore the screen for a Monday-afternoon school-holidays matinee of *Lassie Come Home*, and then remove the screen and restore the set for the play's first night on the Monday. To this day I remember the thirty-six people who turned up to help effect this change at 4 pm, including several hands from farms whose owners had taken pity on our plight, and all was ready and in place with two hours to spare. It always seemed to me to epitomise the community spirit which was so impressive about the place. And the actors themselves: most had never acted before, but it was immensely rewarding to see the sorts of talent and dedication they brought to the task. They accepted the fact that it wasn't enough for them to have fun; it was at least as important for the paying customers to be entertained. Teacher Rex King as an ancient colonel touchingly reminiscing about his late wife in *Waters of the Moon* and legal secretary Ada Carson bravely going

'A *Gibbons Family snap*' *from* This Happy Breed (*Terang, 1956*)

to give herself up to the police in *Ladies in Retirement* are still vivid to me in their understated poignancy fifty-odd years later.

In the remaining year and a third until I went to England in April 1958, I produced a further five plays, finishing with *Waters of the Moon*, a deft enough piece of middle-class social observation by N.C. Hunter, who, perhaps because of his class affiliations, is now rarely heard of, but was in fact a playwright of some real insight within those limitations. Oddly perhaps, directing plays never made me in the least interested in the idea of venturing creatively into *film* production. Possibly the idea of the technology involved would have deterred me, as one who couldn't be counted on to use a box Brownie camera without mishap. When, after seventeen months in England (1958-1959), I returned to Terang in September 1959, a vacancy fortuitously occurring on the High School staff when Johno, my former flatmate, went to Europe, I produced *The Reluctant Debutante*, and in the following year, now married, starred my drama-trained wife Geraldine in two more famously film-adapted theatre successes — *The Heiress*, referred to previously, and *The Philadelphia Story*, one of the sleekest romantic comedy-dramas ever written. It used to be said that one 'made one's own fun' in country towns, but before actually doing so I'd always thought I preferred other people to have done the spadework for my 'fun'. Terang to some extent cured me of that. If it didn't cure me of all character defects, I can only say that this wasn't for lack of brilliant role models and tolerant monitors of youthful excesses.

One of the duties of producer was also to generate the publicity and I was forever taking in 'copy', written in school time and on school paper, to the *Terang Express* about the latest play-reading and the progress of the latest production. The very engaging editor, Len Gallop, would from time to time say to me, 'McFarlane, this is really just free advertising, you know' but would print it just the same — provided I occasionally gave him a paid-for ad. The non-stop publicity, along with following up any hint of interest in drama that came to our ears, no doubt helped the Society's popularity.

Len would very decently give front-page space to the reviews of our productions, reviews written by Gordon Kirby, formerly theatre editor of *Farrago*, my co-editor on *Film Bulletin*, and a well-known Melbourne producer. Kirby, a man of legendary generosity to friends whose name was Legion, at my invitation and that of the producers who succeeded me, used to come down to Terang for each performance. He paid his own fare, no doubt using two days of his annual leave from the State Library, and would sit up writing the very long critique I required until the early hours of the morning, then catch the train at 8.30 am back to Melbourne. In my unmarried years, it never occurred to either my flatmate or me to give up our beds to him, just offering a sort of 'Li-lo' on the floor. In the end, it occurred to *him* that this was no way to treat a critic and he stipulated (a) he was sick of sleeping on the floor, (b) he did not want to be given sausages to eat, and (c) he didn't want to hear 'Greensleeves' (which for some forgotten reason I was addicted to) played in the theatre during interval. We agreed to meet these demanding conditions and various excellent women, hearing about his privations at 8 Warrnambool Road, would invite him — and us — to dine with them before the play. All this was in the interests of securing from him the very long review we wanted for our efforts.

My connection with the *Express* gave me a further chance to write about film as well as about drama. During my time in Terang, the management of the Mechanics Institute underwent a major change and its name metamorphosed to 'The Civic'. It was said, indeed maliciously bruited abroad, that the chairman of the theatre committee had bought up a collection of second-hand neon letters and that 'The Civic' was the only name that could be made from them. Be that as it may, this edifice, under whatever name, was the centre of my extra-curricular life in Terang. At the time of the management changeover, I was talking to its new chairman about the kind of cinema programmes they were screening and he invited me to make a list of what I thought would be the go with local audiences. I doubt if anyone ever took the slightest notice of the list I conscientiously drew up. Well, it was conscientious up to a point: I did include quite a number of titles of films *I* particularly wanted to see and which may not have excited universal anticipation, such as a revival of *A Song to Remember*. However, what was more important to me was that the chairman asked me if I'd like to 'write up' the films on a twice-weekly basis in the *Terang Express*. In return for this, I would be entitled to a free ticket to any screening, in the upstairs section of the theatre to boot. This seemed to me like a perfectly satisfactory salary arrangement: seat tickets in the 'lounge' were 3/6 (35 cents equivalent in those days): I did subsequently wish, though, that I'd held out for a double pass. Still, it was not to be sneezed at, and I didn't, and I would take in my copy to the *Express* office which would print it under my by-line, to a readership no doubt agog with anticipation.

Of course I hadn't seen all the films, though, as a result of sorties to Melbourne at weekends and during school holidays, it was surprising — or not — how many I had. Of those I hadn't seen I would simply give information about the programme, never hesitating to give a boost to old favourites. For example, when *Désirée* came to town, I began my review with the following keenly critical perception: 'The loveliest face ever to appear on the screen? My choice would be Merle Oberon...' Certainly Marlon Brando and Jean Simmons were billed above Merle but I regarded that simply as an aberration that it was almost my duty to correct. And when my old 'mentor' Jill Esmond turned up in a revival of *Random Harvest*, her 'fine character study' (she had all of three minutes of screen time) was duly noted. In my own defence, I should add that I did try to draw urgent attention to films I thought mightn't be adequately known or noticed, such as John Ford's affectionate hymn to the American South, *The Sun Shines Bright*, repeating my *Farrago* eulogy of a year or so earlier. As well, I learnt how to convey my sense of a film's deficiencies without actually spelling them out in a way that would not have been helpful to 'The Civic's' box-office. Instead of belabouring the film, I'd simply place it generically, give a brief suggestion of its plot, and comment on the kinds of talents, before and behind the camera that were of possible interest. This was also roughly the approach I took to the films I hadn't seen. This was clearly not high-level criticism but it slaked some of my thirst for writing about film, which was what I most wanted to do. It was probably partly tied up with the egoistic urge to influence other people's opinions and habits. It was certainly also connected with the need I'd felt since the age of ten to get my own views set down on paper, as if I couldn't know what I thought until I'd seen what I wrote.

When, back from England and married, Geraldine and I were living there during the first year of our married life, in 1960 several of us also started the Terang Film Society. Having been secretary of the Dramatic Society, I decided this time it would be easier to be president and left the serious work of organisation to the secretary. My main responsibility was to write the programme notes for the likes of *Song of Ceylon* (the sort of documentary title no self-respecting film society would have dared omit), the Italian *Bread, Love and Dreams* with the notably voluptuous Gina Lollobrigida (though naturally art was our preoccupation) and Laurence Olivier's *Henry V.* Look at those titles: a documentary, a foreign-language job, and a Shakespearean adaptation. No one could say we weren't trying, though it is true that our screenings in a tiered classroom at the High School never constituted a serious threat to 'The Civic'.

During these Terang years, I was frequently spending weekends and holidays in Melbourne, where I saw films I would write about when they made their way to rural centres. Another bonus of being in Melbourne so often was the possibility of seeing yet more of those legendary names (legendary to me, anyway) on stage where they were probably marginalising local aspirants to theatrical fame. As well as Marsha Hunt, there were Roger Livesey (star of several Michael Powell films, including *The Life and Death of Colonel Blimp, A Matter of Life and Death* and *I Know Where I'm Going!*) and wife Ursula Jeans in *The Reluctant Debutante*, which we subsequently produced in Terang. There were also Dulcie Gray (popular

FILM PREVIEW

(By BRIAN McFARLANE)

Exotic entertainment will be provided by United Artists' Technicolor romantic drama of the South Seas, "Return to Paradise," to be screened at Terang next Wednesday night.

Gary Cooper, seeking a peaceful existence in the Samoan Islands, comes into conflict with an autocratic missionary who goes to fanatical lengths to force the islanders to live by strict moral codes.

Cooper falls in love with an island girl who dies giving birth to his child. Years later, Cooper returns to the island to find his daughter, now grown up, infatuated with an American flyer, and he decides he must stay and protect her.

Roberta Haynes and Moira McDonald, two newcomers, play Cooper's mistress and daughter respectively; noted English character actor Barry Jones plays the missionary and John Hudson the flyer.

The supporting film, "Blue Blood," is a refreshing horseracing drama starring Billy Williams, Jane Nigh, Audrey Long and Arthur Shields.

Samples from Terang Express, 1957

FILM PREVIEW

(By BRIAN McFARLANE)

Few films of recent years have stirred such interest, controversy and widely divergent opinions as "Rock Around the Clock." Few have been such enormous financial block-busters.

In a few years it may be no more than an historical cinematic oddity, but at the moment it commends vast audiences, comprised, one assumes, largely of rock 'n' rolling teenagers and others interested to discover the nature of this craze which has led sections of the nation's youth to such excesses.

The plot behind "Rock Around the Clock" is slight enough. It combines the promotion of a rock 'n' roll orchestra, lead by Bill Haley, and a triangular romance between the promoter (played by singer Johnny Johnston), the business manager of the band (pretty Lisa Gaye) and an old girl friend of the promoter (Alix Tilton). The latter proves rather a snag for a time, but there are no prizes for guessing the outcome.

However, the story is unimportant. It is the exhibitions of roc 'n' roll and the accompanying music which have taken the film to box-office success and it is these which are the film's vital interest. Other participants include Henry Slate and Allen Freed. "Rock Around the Clock" will undoubtedly attract large audiences.

Reliable oldtimer Pat O'Brien heads the cast of "Inside Detroit," the ganster thriller which supports "Rock Around the Clock." A bomb is thrown into an auto workers' hall, killing some men, including the president's brother. This is the starting point for the drama of the film which co-stars Dennis O'Keefe and Margaret Field.

British film star often seen with husband Michael Denison in the 1940s) in *Tea and Sympathy*, Margaret Rutherford (beloved British eccentric) in *The Happiest Days of Your Life*, Judith Anderson in and as *Medea*, Sybil Thorndike and Lewis Casson back again for *The Chalk Garden*, and John McCallum and wife Googie Withers, in *Simon and Laura* and *The Deep Blue Sea*. The McCallums went on to settle in Australia, after illustrious careers in Britain on stage and screen (was there ever a more striking actress in British films than Googie?), and adorned many a stage production here for the next forty years, and became valued friends. These were all people who came trailing clouds of theatrical glory, but to me they were essentially names I revered from their *films*, and getting to know some of them in later years was one of the great pleasures in life.

With all the foregoing activity in Terang and the regular injections of metropolitan high life (as it seemed to me), along with the most extraordinarily hospitable entertainment provided by kind women who didn't think young men could properly feed themselves, there wasn't a great deal of time left available for actual teaching. The school was where I made my living and there was enough good company to make it enjoyable. I still remember with great affection the very cheerful school secretary, Margie Thompson (now Wadelton), who would darn socks (remember darning?) for Johno and me, only stipulating that they had to be washed, saying firmly she would not mend them 'off the hoof'. In the office she shared with the headmaster was the only phone in the school, and Mr Sainsbury and she bore with equanimity the time I would spend on it while casting the next play-reading. I've sometimes spared a pang for all those students who might have had more devoted attention than I was able — or at least, ready — to give. I met some of them again at the fiftieth anniversary of the High School in 1999 and was touched by how kindly their memories had blotted out my skimpy approach to their education. They were very good about making posters for the plays and taking bundles of tickets to sell, and some of them even passed their exams.

Chapter Five
The Great World, sort of ...

n March 1958, on the day I was being farewelled in Terang, the Norwegian ship, the *Skaubryn*, sank in the Indian Ocean. The proud boast of the shipping line that owned it was that only one life was lost and this belonged to an old man with a weak heart to boot: there was almost a suggestion that he was asking for it. The *Skaubryn* had been on its way to Melbourne to collect me and take me to the world in which, as a result of reading and film-viewing, I was so steeped. In the event, most of the passengers booked to travel on the *Skaubryn* were squeezed on to an Italian ship called the *Aurelia*. The fact that the latter was able to take on so many extra bodies at a moment's notice ought to have alerted one to ask something — such as, Why had it been so nearly empty?

The *Aurelia* was a ship rife with rumours: Did you know the bar made £10,000 profit on its last trip? (I wasn't surprised.) Have you heard that we are taking on eighty ballerinas at Perth? (Where would they have been accommodated?) One of the ship's engines gave out during the night? (All too possible.) Its cuisine was limited; the confinement of its public places was extreme; its air-conditioning non-existent; and for thirty-four days one saw the same faces in the same places as the ship dawdled across the Indian Ocean. Nevertheless, a tight little group of us became friends, behaved in what was probably seen as a stand-offish way, lazed about deck and bars, and generally countered potential boredom with the pleasing notion that no one could make us do anything all day (though some tried — and failed — on the day of crossing the Equator when fancy dress was required). An extraordinarily eclectic selection of films was shown on the boat-deck. They included an Audie Murphy boxing tale, *The World in My Corner*, an ancient Bob Hope comedy, *Let's Face It, Brüder Martin* (a biography of Martin Luther) and *The Creature from the Black Lagoon*. Most vividly, I remember peering at Powell and Pressburger's *Black Narcissus* (nunly passions in the Himalayas — or Sussex, as the case really was) round bits of rigging and railing and piping. I have before me, as I write, my judicious assessment of this film I now consider a masterwork as 'Interesting but too leisurely'. All that really interests me about these callow notes is that, indolent as I was on shipboard, I couldn't resist writing them, and there they all are in my carefully preserved diaries which the nation to date has shown no interest in acquiring.

Like many graduates of my vintage, I was intent upon heading to England as soon as possible. 'England' was really a metonym for wider travel but it was very often the first port of call, from which one would make expeditions to 'the Continent'. Europe, with what may now seem an arrogant Old World position of unquestioned superiority, was the only one of the half-dozen or so land masses that one would think of in relation to in this term. I'm not sure that Australian students in the 2000s are in such a rush to head north as my contemporaries were: perhaps there is now less reason for those in search of 'culture' to feel this need: certainly back in the 1950s, almost all my university friends had such travel firmly in mind. (I'm told that New York is now the favoured destination, and I guess it has things going for it.) For those who became teachers with the Education Department, this meant teaching out your 'bond' (very enjoyably in my case in Terang) for three years before booking your passage — and acquiring enough money not just for the passage but to support you on arrival. Some had jobs lined up in advance; others, like me, supposed we'd drift into teaching if nothing better presented itself. The idea was to live as cheaply as possible in matters such as food and rent so as to have plenty to spare for the reasons for being there in the first place. In my case, for six months I slept on the floor of a Hampstead bed-sitting-room inhabited by two other people, one of whom was Don Hewitt, a very old friend of mine from school and university days. They of course had the beds. Every night I would move three cushions from the couch to the floor, blow up a Li-lo and put it on top of these cushions, then get into a sleeping-bag on top of the Li-lo. As the three of us got on amicably, and as my being there meant their rent (£4/10/0 per week altogether) was reduced from a half each to a third we were all quite happy with this austere arrangement. And, anyway, it was worth a little discomfort to live in Hampstead, which, among its other charms, had the famous art-house cinema, the Everyman, which still exists though it now offers more mainstream fare.

London, more broadly speaking, was for me then, and possibly still is, the centre of the known world, and within ten minutes of arriving at Victoria Station I realised that, but for an accident of birth, this was where I was always meant to have been. To fund my life there, I was ultimately, having wasted my not-too-substantial substance in the first few months of dizzy delights, forced to seek paid employment. The pleasure of recognising so many street names from the Monopoly board was somewhat dimmed by their unwillingness to accept Monopoly currency. In answer to several applications in which I represented myself as one of Australia's most caring educators, I was finally invited to an interview at Bec Grammar School, Tooting Bec (what kind of a name was that? I could only wonder) in South London. This was in answer to an ad for English and History staff, and I offered myself in both capacities, deciding it was best not to mention French, placed as they were so near the source of the real thing. In any case, the interviewers were taken aback by my versatility in offering two subjects, UK teachers in those days having as a rule 'read' in only one subject discipline, and I was jocularly referred to as the 'ambidextrous' applicant. They went on to ask how I'd feel about taking Religious Studies, and, needing a job, I agreed at once, then, minutes later, retreated from this unwarranted confidence. I suspect that this is what led the Headmaster to write in a reference I've always kept: 'He may appear diffident in interview but is in fact more competent than he may seem'. A modest recommendation perhaps, it was nevertheless much better than being described as *less* competent than you'd seemed, I felt.

As in Terang, I was not able to spare much time for actual teaching, and this was a shame really because Bec Grammar School, destination for victors of the then-threatening Eleven Plus exams, was a very well-run school and it's not exaggerating to say that it more than reconciled me to the idea of teaching as a profession. This was more a matter of the example of dedicated and civilised colleagues than of my throwing myself into my work. As I said, I couldn't spare too much time on this and probably regarded my daily to and fro journeys from Hampstead as a couple of hours that could be put down to professional duties. At the staff meeting on the first day of the new term, 8 September 1958, the Headmaster, Mr Hore, mentioned that we were all to keep a wary eye on Wayne in 4g as he'd stabbed a class-mate last term. As I was down to teach 4g, I resolved to keep a wary eye out for Wayne. In spite of my corner-cutting approach to lesson-preparation and assignment-marking, I managed to get through the year's teaching without scarring of any kind and to give a very decent impersonation of one whose discipline was irrefragable. Rugby supervision, sometimes on a bleak Saturday afternoon, was an unattractive incursion into the serious part of my life, as were other extra-curricular activities, but I was treated with friendliness and understanding by staff. I was, for instance, let off appearing at the second night of the school's performance of *Noyes Fludde* (I had some minor backstage function) because it was the only night I could get tickets to see Joan Sutherland sing *Lucia di Lammermoor* at Covent Garden. Or on the morning when, having slept through the alarm after a heavy night's entertainment, I arrived at school at 10.30 where I met the Head, Freddie Hore, on my way in, and he was so amiable about it that, slack as I was, I at once resolved not to be guilty of this again. Freddie, a likable and urbane man, became a friend and remained so until his death fifty years later.

But grateful as I was, and must always be, to Bec ('teaching there has been infinitely more rewarding than I should have thought possible', I wrote in my diary), this was not what I was in London for. Re-reading diaries of the period (and don't think this is easy — the fulsomeness, the gravely foolish opinionatedness, the sheer *youthfulness* of their entries! And far too many !s) I'm amazed at the energy I had to dispose of. Certainly, there was no other time like it in my life: to be young and with no responsibilities other than to aim for maximum enjoyment was surely a matter of high privilege. Indeed, 'To be young was very heaven', as Wordsworth noted in other more elevated circumstances. There was, it seemed, a never-ending series of landmarks whose names were familiar from literature and film: in London alone, you couldn't walk ten paces without stumbling on Trafalgar Square or Hyde Park or Charing Cross or Waterloo Bridge or Fortnum and Mason's and dozens of others. Leave London for the countryside, you came across Porlock, of 'Kubla Khan' infamy, or the Doone Valley, or Hardy's 'Wessex', or large towns such as Bath (Jane Austen evoked at every turn) or Norwich (Edith Cavell's touchingly plain grave behind the wonderful Norman Cathedral) or Stratford (you know whom). This isn't a travel book or an autobiography, so I won't go on about the inexhaustible pleasures of drifting round London or England at large, let alone France, Italy (with castles 'precipice-encurled' — a Browning reference duly recorded in my diary to show my education hadn't been entirely wasted) and the rest, including Worms Cathedral, site of Luther's heresy trial and his defiant proclamation, 'Here I stand, I can do no other. God help me.' As well as places, I'm struck in re-reading these embarrassing volumes of diary at the vast network of *people* one knew 'abroad' in those days; not just Australians, though there were plenty of them certainly, but spreading out in ways very congenial to one with so strongly gregarious a streak as I had. It was particularly valuable to have access to flats in Finchley or wherever gaggles of young women ('girls' as they used to be called before feminism was invented) were sharing accommodation and getting on with cooking in ways that escaped most young men ('young men' was what *we* were called, not *boys*). In this way, I even occasionally came across vegetables and other health foods that enabled me to keep up the energy necessary for pursuing a life of unbridled hedonism.

What I was really there for, apart from acquiring a general sense of being immensely cultivated, was the business of seeing as much theatre and cinema as possible — and recording these experiences, not merely as part of the day-to-day action but as well in a special book given over entirely to reviews. New York's 'Broadway' was glitzier but we all knew that London's 'West End' was the world centre of Anglophone theatre. London for me meant many things, but perhaps most of all it meant going to the theatre as much as possible to see in the flesh all those people whose careers I'd been following for years in films. I certainly intended to meet Jill Esmond who had given me such a radical insight into the way things were in the world when I saw her in *My Pal Wolf*. And I did. But this idiosyncratic intention apart, up there on the stage, other than such obvious greats as Gielgud and Edith Evans, Redgrave and Ashcroft, were the film character players to whom I'd become addicted — for instance, mean-faced Raymond Huntley, forever playing the sort of bank manager who, with a vestigial smile, would turn down your request for a loan, or Dora Bryan, blonde floozie or spiteful hussy of dozens of films that often didn't deserve her. I knew from reading *Picture Show* and *Picturegoer* that these five-minute delights in films were often to be found much more prominently cast on the London stage. That films, in fact, were for so many English actors the icing on the cake, as Dora Bryan actually described it to me, and that their first allegiance was to the theatre, a matter confirmed several decades later when I was interviewing about 150 people who had — or once had — careers in British cinema.

In hindsight, I realise that I was in London during a transitional period in English theatre. In their diverse ways, the two seminal plays of the mid-fifties had been *Waiting for Godot* (1955) and *Look Back in Anger* (1956). These had introduced crucial new strands of, respectively, absurdism and realism, in the process appearing to shake up the established modes of drama and comedy represented by the likes of Noël Coward and Terence Rattigan. I say 'appearing to' because decades later Osborne and Harold Pinter would acknowledge Coward at least. In 1958-1959, though, Coward and Rattigan were represented by minor plays which seemed much less exciting to eager seekers after culture than, say, Ionesco's *The Chairs* and *The Lesson*, or Samuel Beckett's *Endgame*, or Arnold Wesker's *Roots*, or Pinter's *The Birthday Party*, or Peter Shaffer's *Five Finger Exercise* or Willis Hall's *The Long and the Short and the Tall*. Some of these were introducing newcomers, such as Joan Plowright and Peter O'Toole, who would become key figures in British film and theatre, but one went to these plays essentially for their *zeitgeist* significance rather than their stars. I mean, one was taking things seriously. Well, up to a point. These new 'young' plays that were supposedly unnerving the establishment and its idea of theatrical entertainment were, of course, not all that was on offer. There were still plenty of musicals, *My Fair Lady* and *West Side Story* most notably, but also a musical adaptation of Ronald Firbank's *Valmouth*, which seemed the last word in sophisticated decadence: it had a cardinal baptising a dog before the high altar of his cathedral! There were also middle-class dramas and comedies set, as of yore, in the Home Counties; there was the last gasp of poetic drama with T.S. Eliot's *The Elder Statesman*; there was the now-forgotten pleasure of revue (e.g., Dora Bryan in *Living for Pleasure*); and, at the highest cultural levels, which we were certainly bent on scaling, there was a steady stream of classic plays, in Stratford as well as London, not to speak of opera and ballet, though I always thought the latter would be speeded up if people would only talk. ('Don't shoot. I'm not really a swan, I'm a princess in disguise', and so on.) Neither before nor since have I ever felt so cultivated: everything was there for the taking, and I took it. And then I wrote about it.

As I said, one of the real pleasures of London theatre-going for me was seeing in the flesh actors I'd known only from films. (Those who fear a list of once-famous actors, many no longer with us, would do well to skip the next two paragraphs.) It was better if they were in good plays (as Wendy Hiller and Ralph Richardson so poignantly were, in Robert Bolt's *Flowering Cherry*) than bad (as Margaret Leighton, in a series of demented costumes by, I see I noted, Norman Hartnell, was in Rattigan's *Variation on a Theme* — 'tawdry', I see I called it then). But though I would be very severe about the 'bad' plays in my reviews (well, what else can I call them, even if I was their sole reader?), I wouldn't have dreamt of not going to unpromising titles if, say, Vivien Leigh and Claire Bloom, plus Freda Jackson, the great harridan of British films, were starring in Giradoux's mannered, windy *Duel of Angels*, or Peter Finch in a boring American two-hander, William Gibson's *Two for the See-saw*, or a pride of character players in such justly-forgotten farces as *Breath of Spring*, with cast led by Athene Seyler, Mary Merrall, Joan Sims and Michael Shepley, or *Caught Napping*, with wintry-faced Raymond Huntley and 1930s Aldwych star of stage and screen, Winifred Shotter, or *Gilt and Gingerbread*, starring John Clements and Kay Hammond, and introducing Richard Briers as a manic young engineer. Jean Kent, so long admired as the sexy bad girl of Gainsborough melodramas, had one great moment in a soppy musi-cal called *Marigold*, based on an old play which had once starred Sophie Stewart, who turned up in a supporting role in the musical version. Legendary beauty Gladys Cooper, getting her 'round' when she first appears on a stepladder pruning roses, graced a silly play, *The Bright One*, pseudonymously written by actress Judy Campbell, and directed by Rex Harrison as a gesture to his then-terminally ill wife, the luminous film star, Kay Kendall. And Sybil Thorndike and Lewis Casson did what they could with Clemence Dane's *Eighty in the Shade*, which I pronounced 'enjoyable enough but no more than a vehicle for the Cassons'.

Fortunately it wasn't always a matter of having to make do with famous stars or well-loved character plays propping up inferior proj-ects. There were, for instance, Flora Robson and Donald Wolfit doing a spell-binding *Ghosts*, and Celia Johnson and Hugh Williams dealing gracefully with a graceful comedy, *The Grass Is Greener*, which Williams had co-written with his Australian ex-actress wife, Margaret Vyner. Your reviewer felt the latter, an 'entirely delightful comedy', displayed 'an easy confidence in the writing which inspires a similar confidence in the audience', finishing the review with 'I look forward to the Williamses' next'. They'd have been so heartened by that. Charles Laughton (Charles Laughton!) did a bravura turn in Jane Arden's *The Party*, which also brought Albert Finney to West End notice in what now seems to have been a symbolic meeting of two acting traditions, and Diana Wynyard starred in the 'well-made' middle-class drama, NC Hunter's *A Touch of the Sun*, supported by arch purveyor of drawing-room suavity, Ronald Squire, and willowy Hollywood import, Louise Allbritton, whom I met for a few entertaining minutes. Vanessa Redgrave also made her London debut in this; her father Michael had vacated the play by the time I saw it and was playing in and as *Hamlet* at Stratford with Googie Withers and Dorothy Tutin as Gertrude and Ophelia respectively, while Dorothy Tutin was also playing Viola in *Twelfth Night*, 'achieving moments [I wrote] of finely controlled pathos, and at other times revealing a charming sense of fun'. That was true I think, and less cringe-making than my encomium to Gladys Cooper: 'She is one of the glories of the English stage and long may she grace it in better plays than this [*The Bright One*]'.

If seeing film stars and film character actors in the flesh was one of the highest priorities of my London life, then this youthful zeal was never better rewarded than at the Palladium's *Night of a 100 Stars*, an annual midnight theatrical charities revue. In the 1959 show, you could have seen — and I did — Edith Evans and John Gielgud dance a waltz, Michael Redgrave and Peggy Ashcroft a polka, and (prior to what looked like a blazing row in the wings, visible from my side-circle seat) Margaret Leighton and Laurence Harvey a Charleston. As well as other Great Names of the Theatre — Ralph Richardson, Beatrice Lillie (trimming the claws of a lobster with her nail scissors, and painting her own nails with an asparagus stick, in a restaurant sketch), Paul Scofield, Margaret Rawlings and dozens of others, all welcomed by Laurence Olivier as host of the cabaret-set second half — were some spectacular *film* stars. There were Audrey Hepburn and Elizabeth Taylor — were there bigger stars in the world then? — and their consorts, Mel Ferrer and Eddie Fisher, Paul Robeson, whose well-known leftist opinions cost him the applause of the Ferrers, I am sorry to add, my father's favourite Bob Hope, and any number of British favourites including Phyllis Calvert, Dulcie Gray and Michael Denison, Sylvia Syms, Richard Attenborough, Joan Greenwood and Robert Morley, and up-coming pop star, Tommy Steele. Many of these simply came on stage, shook the Olivier hand or kissed the Olivier cheek, while we in the audience happily applauded this spectacle. I could name dozens more, but fear to risk boring those who've already read enough names. The first half had made more of a pretence at a programme, for example in the dances suggested above, but essentially it was a night for the star-struck to look at the stars and be stricken. A well-placed bomb could have wiped out the British entertainment world.

I saw film people not just on the stage but also sometimes on television, though these sightings were confined to visits in better appointed houses than any I could afford to have rented. There were Flora Robson in a long-forgotten 'colour problem' drama called *The Untouchable*, loftily judged as 'superficial but still very watchable', Jean Kent, Guy Rolfe and Margaret Johnston in something called *The Sulky Fire*, Michael Hordern and Brenda Bruce in John Mortimer's *What Shall We Tell Caroline?*, none of these considered significant enough to register in any of the filmographies of the actors concerned, but preserved in my diary entries. As well as on stage and TV, poetry recitals were another site of display for those previously only known to me on film: Flora Robson again and Robert Harris did a Sunday night reading of (mainly) the Metaphysical Poets in the Orangery at Kenwood House, Hampstead; elegant Margaret Rawlings, who'd only done a couple of films (*Roman Holiday*, for one), together with Alan Wheatley (memorably killed in an early scene from *Brighton Rock*) performed at Festival Hall, as did Joyce

Grenfell, toothy delight of many an English comedy; while Marius Goring (of *The Red Shoes* and other Powell and Pressburger triumphs) read from the Romantic Movement for the Apollo Society. Because Nicolette Bernard, his co-reader was a friend of Gerie's (by this point my fiancée), we got to meet Mr Goring briefly afterwards, and thirty years later I interviewed him for a book I was doing, interested to find that this vaguely sinister 'foreign'-seeming actor was, in fact, wholly English. And *forty* years later I wrote the *Dictionary of National Biography* entry on him.

But you could also occasionally just see film faces in the street. As a Victoria League visitor, I was in Windsor for the Garter ceremony at the Castle, and looked after by a breathless young woman who introduced herself as Ann, Duchess of Roxburgh, who apologised for the lateness of my host, Sir William Adeane, who was delayed lunching with the Queen. If I'd known he was the Queen's secretary, I'd have been more careful not to call him Sir Michael. But that's beside the main point: in the street, after the ceremony, a friend who lived locally pointed out Ealing stalwart Frederick Piper and Mary Kerridge, both often seen in plays at the Royal Windsor, walking past us, my friend not feeling this was a matter of much interest. Not to him, anyway. Or you might notice Michael Wilding urbanely at large in the Strand, or Robert Morley, large and urbane, in the foyer of the Queen's Theatre where Gielgud's *Ages of Man* was the attraction. If you were bold enough, you could ask to meet an actor backstage, and that was how I first met Dora Bryan, who offered me a slice of the apricot pie someone had given her. A line from one of her songs has stayed with me: 'There's nothing quite so out of date as tarts with hearts of gold,' which she sang for me thirty-two years later when I interviewed her.

Jill Esmond deserves a paragraph to herself. Since she first inducted me into the differences between art and life in *My Pal Wolf*, I've seen her in many films and am always impressed with the unfussy naturalism of her acting. This is true even of some early 1930s films when theatre people, including her then-husband

81

Laurence Olivier, couldn't be counted on not to seem too 'big' for the screen's relentless scrutiny. However, excellent actress and under-valued as I thought her, it was really that afternoon at a children's matinee in a cinema in up-country Victoria that taught me the valu-able lesson about acting and its bearing on the art/life dichotomy. I guess it could easily have been someone else who performed this signal function, but the fact remained that it *was* Jill, and at 6 pm on Sunday 3 August 1958 (I've checked this in a diary; I can't say that the *date* was emblazoned on my mind) I presented myself at her invitation at her house in Queen's Grove, St John's Wood, for a drink. The other guests were the distinguished actor George Relph (father of production designer/producer Michael and grandfather of producer Simon, both of whom I'd meet decades later) and his wife, actress Mercia Swinburne, and the conversation in the garden ranged widely and casually over the great names of the English the-atre — Edith, Johnnie, Gladys, Gwen, etc, and several references by Jill to Larry, whom she once endearingly described as a 'silly arse'. They were all nicely and unpatronisingly interested in Australia, which Relph had visited with Olivier and the Old Vic Company in the late 1940s, but I was really more interested in what *they* were more familiar with.

On subsequent visits to London, I had more chance to talk to Jill about her own film career, on the subject of which she was inclined to be self-deprecating. She became our friend and we would never have thought of being in London without seeing her. By this time, the mid 1970s, she had moved to Southfields, near Wimbledon, and she would regale us, at my instigation, with tales of her times in Hollywood: first in the early 1930s when her film career was moving faster than Olivier's, then in the war years with a young son, when she and other members of Hollywood's British colony would lend moments of authenticity to precariously English-set dramas such as *The White Cliffs of Dover* (a wartime flag-waver which made its way to my Victorian country town some years after there was any war to wave for). She recalled Gary Cooper's solicitude for her then-elderly mother, actress Eva Moore, who fell ill in Hollywood when Jill was in Cooper's comedy, *Casanova Brown*. In England in 1931, she'd very much liked working for Hitchcock in *The Skin Game*, a stagy adaptation of Galsworthy's play, in which she almost alone does not look stagy. She was a woman of courage and style, whose life was not notably easy, and I think a remark of hers which suggests as well real generosity of spirit was her answer to a comment of my wife's about Peter Brook's production of *Midsummer Night's Dream*: 'Oh, for me, I think I'll always regard Vivien Leigh's Titania at the Old Vic [1937] as how the *Dream* should be done'. She stopped acting in the mid 1950s, was active in theatrical charities and in her last years was bedevilled with ill-health, but remained shrewd, amusing and instructive company. I dedicated a book to her memory in 1992 as a small thank-you for the lesson she had inadvertently taught me, and in recognition of a rewarding friendship.

Jill Esmond, 1930s (above)
1940s (right)

Bearing in mind that in 1958 television had scarcely made an impact in Australia, certainly not if you were living in rural Victoria as I had been, the only hope there was of seeing famous films of the past was at the odd revival screening in the capital cities. (There may also have been film societies doing their bit in this respect but I had no access to these.) As well, there were newer titles and foreign classics that eluded me in Terang, and London was awash with irresistible temptations in all these categories. There was a weekly journal called *What's On* which I would scan on my way from Hampstead to Bec and mark off the entertainments I planned to pursue in the ensuing week. The main sites of such film-going were the National Film Theatre (NFT), under Waterloo Bridge, where I remember vividly on one occasion booking seats for twenty-seven films to come in the next month or so, art-houses such as Hampstead's Everyman or Oxford Street's Academy Cinema, and, dotted over London, little 'Classic Cinemas' which, in pre-TV days, did a thriving business by showing all sorts of famous films that had never before come my way in Australia. I'd for instance never seen Orson Welles's masterpieces *Citizen Kane* and *The Magnificent Ambersons*, until catching them at the Baker Street Classic, or *The Petrified Forest* (Kilburn Classic), starring an ardent young Bette Davis and dangerous young Humphrey Bogart, or the flamboyant MGM Dickens adaptations of the 1930s, *David Copperfield* and *A Tale of Two Cities* (NFT), let alone such silent film classics as *The Cabinet of Dr Caligari*, *The Scarlet Letter* with Lillian Gish playing Hawthorne's tragic heroine, and D.W. Griffith's multi-storied, epoch-making *Intolerance* (all at the NFT). The wealth of foreign language films shown at the Everyman and the Academy — seasons of Ingmar Bergman and Jean Renoir, along with new Polish films such as Andrzej Wajda's *Kanal* and *Ashes and Diamonds* — meant that it was effortlessly possible to become cine-literate. You needed to be able to speak of Bergman without anyone's supposing for a moment that you meant Ingrid rather than Ingmar. All the viewings of this year and a half were faithfully and fearlessly critiqued in my journals, still unpublished after all this time. What with all this *richesse*, along with keeping up with new films and those other cultural treats sketched above, you can see how difficult it was for me to set aside time for my paid employment.

But this irresponsible pursuit of pleasure could not have lasted indefinitely. Geraldine (Gerie) my girlfriend, later fiancée, then (and, fifty years later, still) wife couldn't believe that anyone with so little money could see so many plays and films. She still can't. She has, though, for some time accepted the fact that I *need* to see a lot of films and to write about them, only occasionally suggesting that I've succeeded in making my hobby my work so that no one can accuse me of idling. I'm not either, and the evidence of those long-ago journals makes clear how seriously — not to say solemnly — I engaged in this activity. I had first seen her (as Geraldine Burston) on the stage of the Union Theatre at the University of Melbourne and took the precaution of giving her a rave review in *Farrago* as Mrs Erlynne in *Lady Windermere's Fan* (1955), the second time I saw her. What I actually wrote in *Farrago* included the following:

> But perhaps the most exciting feature of the evening was the performance of Geraldine Burston, hitherto glimpsed only briefly in "The Admirable Crichton." She brought real warmth, dignity and poignancy to the role of Mrs. Erlynne, with her heart aching, and her head planning, for a return to the respectability of the London society which ostracised her many years before.
>
> She looked magnificent, wearing her period clothes to perfection, carried herself with a distinctive poise and ease, and spoke her lines with a feeling born of complete understanding. What genuine emotional feeling the play achieved redounds very largely to her credit.

We met just once more after this before running into each other in the Hampstead Post Office (she'd just come to live in a flat a couple of blocks from where I was) on 27 September 1958. I thereafter pursued her with more relentlessness than subtlety, her flatmate suggesting she was being too available to my invitations. From September 1958, the diary entries are full of references to her, and, no, I'm not going to quote them here. Ambitiously I organised a party of six — three women and three men, including one it turned out she was rather taken by — to go to Norway for a fortnight's skiing over Christmas. Well, the party dwindled till there were only Gerie, a university friend, Margaret Stohr, and I left. On the boat to Bergen was a large British colonial party whose hearty leader was called Trevor: I was very moved when Gerie and Margaret unanimously elected me the leader of *our* party. My first act in this exalted position was to get us off at the wrong station in snowbound Norway, owing to the similarity of two names, and we then had to be taken by sled from the cosy pension I'd brought us to and on to our Youth Hostel destination. Australians did not emerge well at the New Year festivities when Youth of All Nations were performing national song and dance. We could only come up with a defectively-remembered rendering of 'A Bush Christening' with actions. Most of the audience was mystified and Gerie and I retired to drink duty-free brandy to numb our recollections.

Anyway, I knew about courtship from the films, where it always ended happily, so I persisted, and finally broke her will, and persuaded her (in Paris, to be exact) to ally herself with me permanently. We got engaged in Paris, after the first substantial meal I'd treated her to in over a week (could she have agreed out of sheer gratitude?), and clinched this with a ring bought in Vienna, with money borrowed from a friend. I think that's exotic enough. Also in Vienna, remembering MGM's *The Great Waltz*, with Miliza Korjus trilling away, I felt we needed to visit the real Vienna Woods, and spent an hour or so slithering around in the mud, trying to sing at the same time. Slender, dark-haired and with more than a passing resemblance to Merle but with a mind and a humour distinctly her own, Gerie had been studying acting at the Central

Geraldine Burston

School of Speech and Drama for a year. However, she'd decided not to continue after the first year though invited to do so. When we re-met, she was thinking of returning to Australia within six months. That would have been without me, and who knows what competitors would have sought to displace me. I'd been planning to come home later in 1959 via America, but scrapped that idea when I needed the money to repay my friend for the loan to buy the ring in Vienna. We finally returned to Melbourne together in August 1959, with awe-inspiring numbers of family members for each to be presented to. As I said in the previous chapter, I was able to go back to Terang High School (and indeed to the same flat), to start earning again. I *needed* to do this as I was living on the residue of £20 borrowed from my sister's husband, and this state of things wasn't very impressive to my future father-in-law when we had a Financial Chat. We were finally married in Melbourne on 27 February 1960 and spent the first year of married life happily in Terang. Life was about to become more serious, but in the months between getting engaged and leaving London, there was a long, spectacularly rainless and beautiful summer, much of which we spent wandering over Hampstead Heath, and fifty years later this remains one of our favourite memories.

A Wimmera vista, 2008, from what was our front gate

Nhill Memorial Theatre, early 1950s

Nhill Memorial Community Centre, 2008 (still used for screenings)

Souvenir Programme, 1945

A hero brought to book, 1999

Early Picture Show *purchases*

Early Picturegoer
purchases

Picturegoer, 1947

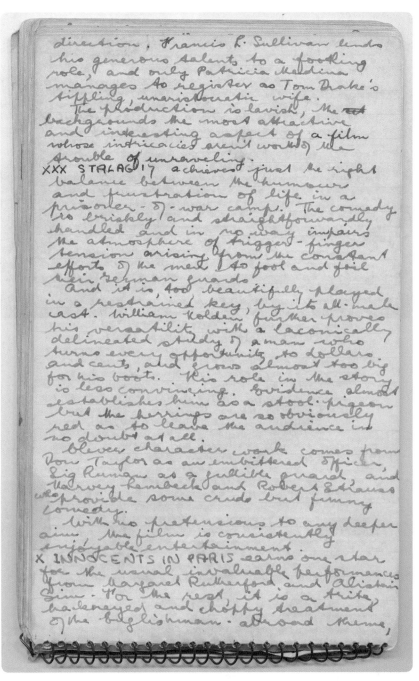

direction; Francis L. Sullivan lends his generous talents to a fooling role, and only Patricia Medina manages to register as Tom Drake's tippling, unaristocratic wife.

The production is lavish, the backgrounds the most attractive and interesting aspect of a film whose intricacies aren't worth the trouble of unraveling.

XXX STALAG 17 achieves just the right balance between the humour and frustration of life in a prisoner-of-war camp. The comedy is briskly and straightforwardly handled and in no way impairs the atmosphere of trigger-finger tension arising from the constant efforts of the men to fool and foil their German guards.

And it is, too, beautifully played in a restrained key, by its all-male cast. William Holden further proves his versatility with a laconically delineated study of a man who turns every opportunity to dollars and cents, and grows almost too big for his boots. His role in the story is less convincing. Evidence almost establishes him as a stool-pigeon but the herrings are so obviously red as to leave the audience in no doubt at all.

Clever character work comes from Don Taylor as an embittered officer, Sig Ruman as a gullible guard, and Harvey Lembeck and Robert Strauss who provide some crude but funny comedy.

With no pretensions to any deeper aim, the film is consistently enjoyable entertainment.

X INNOCENTS IN PARIS earns one star for the usual invaluable performances from Margaret Rutherford and Alastair Sim. For the rest, it is a trite, hackneyed and choppy treatment of the Englishman-abroad theme,

Still a very young critic, at work in 1954

Starting to take life seriously, 1961…

…and some of the results:
Duncan (with Henrietta and Dougall),
Sophie (with Ben and Declan),
Susannah (with Emma and Edvard)

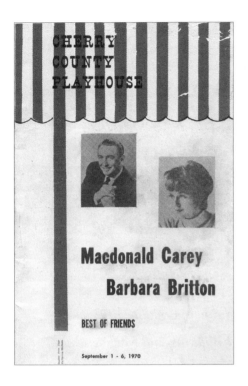

Programme for Traverse City's summer theatre, 1970

Merle Oberon by her pool, Acapulco, 1970. Taken with a shaky hand by the author.

At the Sixty Voices *launch, London, 1992*
Above: Marius Goring, Roy Boulting and Michael Ralph
Below: Kathleen Byron, Jean Kent, Dora Bryan and Muriel Pavlow

*Valerie Hobson
also at the* Sixty Voices
launch

*John McCallum
and Googie
Withers. Friends.*

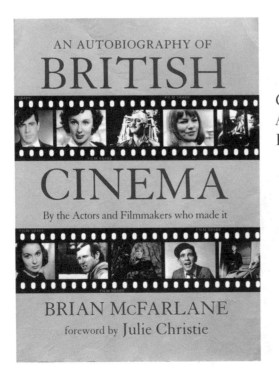

Gathering them up:
An Autobiography of
British Cinema, 1997

Putting it all together:
The Encyclopedia
of British Film,
2003/05/08/10

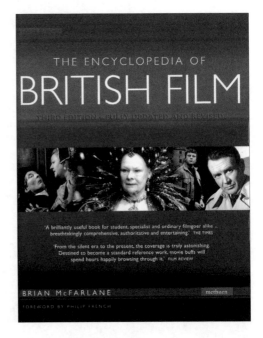

Chapter Six
The importance of being earnest

The 1960s were essentially a matter of Settling Down and Getting On, the post-marriage year together in Terang being almost entirely a matter of, as Lady Bracknell said, 'living for pleasure'. There was, increasingly, much concern with earning a living. Recalling that chat I'd had with my father-in-law-to-be about The Future, I didn't want him to feel his daughter had taken up with someone feckless. I mean, I *had* been feckless, if spending all your substance on the manifold delights of London is feckless, but I was now prepared to become a solid citizen. More or less. And getting a job at Trinity Grammar School, Kew, as its first master-in-charge of English, was considerably better than my spotty employment record might have entitled me to expect. I suspect I was helped to this post by the good offices of Margot Westerton, who ran the agency supplying non-government schools with staff and who was an old chum of the great Mollie Bennett in Terang. The Headmaster, John Leppitt, interviewed me while we stood under a large Moreton Bay fig tree, half-watching whatever was going on out on the oval. His respect for Margot was such that he was unlikely to query a recommendation from her — even in relation to one so little deserving of it as I was.

Unlike those previous jobs at Terang and Tooting Bec, this one was going to make serious inroads on my time. The day was by no means over at 4 pm, nor the week on Friday afternoon. Being of a more or less obsessive personality, I was clearly going to cope with the demands of Trinity only by allowing my work there to become yet another obsession in my life. This didn't happen at once or as a matter of conscious decision, but I gradually became aware of its importance in my life, not just as a source of necessary income, though I was sentimentally attached to those monthly cheques, but also as a source of real stimulus. This was particularly so in the matter of teaching Form 6 (later Year 12) Literature, which forced me to focus attention on what had been a too easy and indiscriminate pleasure in reading. For fifteen years, with a year out for an overseas venture in 1970-1971, teaching the 'Lit' class was one of the greatest satisfactions of my life. I think it is true to say that, in all the following twenty-five years spent in tertiary teaching, I never came across classes so steeped in the texts they were studying. Mind you, as a school teacher, I had ways not available to an academic of ensuring that my students had at least *read* their prescribed books, and I had a level of responsibility for this that very properly doesn't exist at tertiary level where students are responsible for themselves. I doubt if I had any theories about the teaching of literature; my general aim was to try to keep students sufficiently interested and entertained so that they wouldn't notice how hard they were working, and it's been a major pleasure to have kept friendly contact with so many of them. They routinely wrote two essays a week, and for those who'd had trouble completing these over the weekend I generously made provision for them to do so after school on Monday. I liked to think they'd be grateful in the end.

Apart from the daily expectation of fronting up to classes with lessons prepared and all that went along with this (and for the first time I was doing this properly), there were other activities that accounted for a lot of time and energy. I got into the way of producing an annual play for Trinity in conjunction with Ruyton, the neighbouring girls' school, starting with Kaufman and Hart's sturdy New Deal comedy, *You Can't Take It with You*, so as not to scare off potential audiences with something of too obviously improving a nature. It had come to my mind as a result of seeing the film version for the first time, on TV, and it seemed to offer a good, manageable range of parts, some sure laughs and a bit of moral uplift at the end. It proved popular with audiences, and among the plays that followed were: Terence Rattigan's equally sturdy matinee drama, *The Winslow Boy*, in which the charismatic Counsel for the Defence, Sir Robert Morton, was aptly played by Miles Kupa, who would later become a senior diplomat and, as I write, is High Commissioner to Singapore; Thornton Wilder's stylised *Our Town*; the famous farce, *The Happiest Days of Your Life*, whose stars, Wilfred Last and Loane Wilson (later Skene), became respectively the first 'Don' of David Williamson's *Don's Party* and Pro-Vice Chancellor of the University of Melbourne; and Anouilh's *The Lark* (starring as Joan of Arc was Susan Rowley, who became Deputy Vice-Chancellor of Sydney's University of Technology), *The Importance of Being Earnest*, *Macbeth* and *Hamlet*. *Macbeth*, a famously unlucky play, lived up to its reputation here. Donalbain left school to join the cast of *Hair* in Sydney; Old Siward broke his arm; and the star went down with glandular fever in the week before performance and the role was then assumed by the staff member who had been helping with the production. This staff member, Terry Hayes, really needed his glasses but these would have been anachronistic, so that for several of the cast with whom he engaged in realistic swordplay that was real fear they were evincing. Amateur play production is something to do when you're very young and energetic, and especially not when you've got small children who haven't mastered the knack of sleeping through the night.

But despite the energies involved in taking a career seriously and in adjusting to the insistent demands of, eventually, three children, the movies never lost their lure, even if it became harder to access them, though television helped to fill a few gaps. It wasn't only a matter of the demands of family life that curtailed my film-going; as well, I returned to study for a Master's Degree at Melbourne University, and because of my lamentable performance as a full-time student twelve years earlier, opting out of my Honours course after two years, I had to do three MA Preliminary subjects and write a thesis (over-ambitiously, on George Eliot). What I did discover during this return to academic study was that the 'work' was really the

most absorbing thing about university life, and I couldn't understand
how I'd failed to notice this back in the early 1950s. I realised I had
some brilliant teachers in these two years of study, including Peter
Steele, Maggie Tomlinson and Vincent Buckley, and some vestige of
late-arriving maturity led me to make the most of them and it. The
subsequent MA thesis on some aspects of Australian literature was
a pretty undistinguished piece of work, but it pointed me in some
directions I found I wanted to go — and I gouged six articles out of
it which helped me to achieve this end.

Film, then, was pushed into the wings for a few years while the
likes of John Donne or Henry James claimed time left over from
Trinity Grammar and the youthful household trinity, which comprised Duncan, Susannah and Sophie, who arrived in 1963, 1965
and 1967 respectively. These three produced the usual share of
infant alarms about health, with panicky rushes out for all-night
chemists and allied excursions, but compensated with a wonder of
devotion that perhaps only small children can show or evoke. And
the way one's weekend activities changed! Regular sorties by me to
local parks and playgrounds on a Saturday afternoon enabled Gerie
to rest and summon the energy for what passed for social life in the
evening. Films, as you can see, had to take a back seat. However,
for well over a decade, my old friend John Fox ('best man' at each
other's wedding, godfather to each other's sons) and I had solemnly
exchanged our 'Best Ten' lists at the end of the year. It was not just
a matter of the films, but also of directors, actors, supporting actors
etc, and a study of these lists would reveal the shrinkage of actual
viewings. My Best Ten films foundered somewhat in 1963 on the
fact that I'd only seen fifteen all up, eight of those before my son
was born in May, including a schools' visit to *Long Day's Journey
into Night,* and a drive-in to see *Birdman of Alcatraz,* while Duncan slept soundly in his carry-cot. My awards for this depleted year
were dominated by *Long Day's Journey* (best film, actor [Ralph
Richardson], actress [Katharine Hepburn's 'dazzlingly controlled
and ruthlessly unsentimental Mary Tyrone' — I had become very

adverbial I note]), but the direction award went to Martin Ritt for *Hud*, 'with affectionate mention for [John] Ford at his best in years with *The Man Who Shot Liberty Valance*'. A Best Ten list based on fifteen films can't perhaps be seen as definitive, and the last paragraph of this letter to Fox suggests reasons for the meagreness: 'Duncan is now v. mobile, has turned on his first gas fire, eaten his first cardboard box, and had his first cold'.

John and I took this annual exchange very seriously and on one occasion at least (1956) he reproved me for not including enough foreign films. Possibly as a result of this, I see that for 1957 my first three were Claude Autant-Lara's *Le Blé en herbe*, Arne Sucksdorff's *The Great Adventure* and René Clair's *Les grandes manoeuvres*: you couldn't get more Continental than that. However, I suspect that during the maximally busy years of the 1960s, my chief aim was to be Taken Out of Myself, though I would never have admitted that at the time. John and I once had a long discussion about Desert Island films; our wives refused to enter into the spirit of this enterprise. His wife, Jan, said that a film would be the last thing she'd take to a desert island, and mine said that, if she was being wrecked on a desert island with John and me, she'd take a film on how to put up a tent. Despite these cynical and uncaring responses, John and I continued until his death in 1996 to share our opinions on the year's offerings: it always provided a focus for our viewings, even when by the mid-1970s I was fairly regularly writing about films in one forum or another. In 1969, I see (from John's carefully preserved letters) I was austerely only allowing seven into the Top Ten: *Accident, 2001: A Space Odyssey, Belle de Jour, Bonnie and Clyde, La Guerre est finie, Romeo and Juliet* and *The Swimmer*, adding 'not in any special order, except that the first four are well ahead of the next three'. Work, including the directing of *Macbeth* and the demands of family life were taking their toll on the crucial business of film-viewing — and at a very important time when Old Hollywood was giving way to new and when there was an extraordinary efflorescence of European cinema, with names such as Ingmar Bergman, Michelangelo

Antonioni and Alain Resnais vying for the attention of the serious-minded likes of John and me.

The other film- and film-writing-related activity I pursued at Trinity was in the formation of a Trinity Film Society for which, quite undemocratically, I chose the films, and for which I wrote the accompanying notes for each screening. A former student, Ian Britain, who later became the editor of Australia's oldest and most prestigious literary journal, *Meanjin*, claimed to have preserved these notes, and in fact located yellowing foolscap sheets with credits and programme notes (see below) rendered on an ancient typewriter. (Mind you, he still has his Year 9 Geography notes and he is now

TRINITY FILM SOCIETY.

presents

as its third screening for 1964

"THE THIRTY-NINE STEPS".

Directed by	Alfred Hitchcock
Produced by	Michael Balcon
Photography by	Bernard Knowles
Based on the novel by	John Buchan

CAST

Hannay. . . .	Robert Donat	Crofter.	John Laurie
Pamela. . . .	Madeleine Carroll	Mrs. Jordan . . .	Helen Haye
Miss Smith . .	Lucie Mannheim	The Sheriff . . .	Frank Cellier
Professor Jordan	Godfrey Tearle	Memory	Wylie Watson
Crofter's Wife .	Peggy Ashcroft	Commercial Travellers	Gus MacNaughton
		. . .	Jerry Verno

¶ This is vintage Hitchcock. Made in 1935, it belongs to the period of his best work, to the days of "The Lady Vanishes" and the first "Man Who Knew Too Much". Some of his more recent films have suffered from the modern tendency to unjustified length, to a rather "sick" revelling in the merely nasty; but in "The Thirty-Nine Steps", we see all the old flair for fast-moving narrative, interlaced with sophisticated comedy touches, swift, incisive character-drawing, and the brilliant, ironic use of natural, everyday settings to heighten the excitement of the events being played out against them. Above all it has the unpretentious liveliness, the relish in good story cleverly told, which has always marked his most entertaining work. "The Sunday Times", in reviewing the film in 1936, wrote:
    "The director has evoked by processes known only to himself a narrative of the unexpected - a humorous, exciting, dramatic, entertaining, pictorial, vivid and novel tale told with a fine sense of character and with a keener grasp of the cinematic idea than is seen in thousands of films aiming at similar objectives."
    The cast, too, is splendid. Robert Donat is an admirable hero, and Madeleine Carroll does prettily by the slender role of the girl who becomes handcuffed to Hannay; but the real delights are in the supporting players: in Godfrey Tearle's bogus professor, in Helen Haye as his enigmatic wife, and the two unnamed actresses as his odd daughters; in Lucie Mannheim as the murdered woman; in Wylie Watson's brief appearance as "Memory", pawn in a spy game; and in the touching little cameo from Peggy Ashcroft as the crofter's wife who helps Hannay.

***

nearer sixty than fifty.) The programme notes were intended to make them knowledgeable and, some would say, pretentious about the films shown. These are perhaps, though, the first of my film writings I can read without too much cringing. On David Lean's *Great Expectations*, I wrote: 'As an adaptation of one of Dickens's best novels, this film should please all but the purists who insist that the film should follow the book in every detail. In fact, the film does keep closely to the original for at least three quarters of its length, and the changes towards the end seem to me of no great moment'. I was interested then in the early 1960s in the business of adaptation which would become one of my main critical pursuits several decades on. Back then, I was still able to write of Lean's *Oliver Twist* that it 'brings faithfully to the screen one of the best-loved books in the language, retaining the spirit and atmosphere of the novel as well as most of its incidents and characters'. Or of George Cukor's *David Copperfield*, that if it 'were filmed today, it would doubtless be given a more "realistic" treatment than MGM gave it in 1935; one can't help feeling that it would lose thereby a good deal of its authentically Dickensian flavour'. Words like 'faithfully' and 'spirit' would need a lot of scrutiny in later decades, prior to being properly dismissed, but I don't think these and other notes misrepresented the films to their young audience.

We didn't show only films derived from Dickens: some of these were chosen because of their connection with books students were studying (e.g., *Oliver Twist*), and possibly for the wrong reason that it would help them with their study of the novel. As well, though, these were interspersed with Hitchcock (*The Lady Vanishes*, *The Thirty-Nine Steps*), the MGM musical *On the Town*, Charles Crichton's Ealing comedy, *The Titfield Thunderbolt* (a title which gave rise to some childish witticisms I was forced to disdain), and the Marx Brothers classic *A Night at the Opera*. Of the Hitchcock, I was then taking the now unfashionable view that these represented his best work, noting that *The Thirty-Nine Steps* displayed 'all his old flair for fast-moving narrative, interlaced with sophisticated comedy touches, swift, incisive character-drawing, and the brilliant, ironic use of natural, everyday settings to heighten the excitement of the events being played out against them. Above all, it has the unpretentious liveliness, the relish in a good story cleverly told, which has always marked his most entertaining work'. All right, *Vertigo* and *Psycho* are more 'important', but some of the later films achieve importance at the cost of that 'unpretentious liveliness'. I also used these programme notes to proselytise on behalf of the character actors I so enjoyed, such as majestic Margaret Dumont 'whose vulnerability to Groucho's lascivious overtures and whose desperate attempts to preserve her dignity at all costs add much to the joys of the best of the Brothers' bedlam' in *A Night at the Opera*. These 16mm films were screened in a then-scruffy school hall by a couple of technology-mad students, and there was no guarantee that there would not be intervals during which this pair made on-the-spot repairs to the projectors and I attempted to keep the audience happy with 'background information' about the film in question.

This was a time — the 1960s — when film was not a regular, or even irregular, item on the secondary school curriculum, though the idea of 'film culture' was beginning to gain ground in the larger world. The flood of books on film-related topics was underway by the later 60s, and there was even a bookshop in Melbourne, called 'Space Age' which was wholly devoted to such works. My students at Trinity probably had more exposure to film than their counterparts in many other such schools, secondary-school students being more or less at the mercy of their teachers' addictions. Film was barely respectable as a subject for serious study, but there were ways of sneaking it into English and the lives of the impressionable young. For instance, and I can't now remember on what grounds I justified this, I took an entire Year 9 to see a revival of *Gone with the Wind* at a Melbourne city cinema. In the mid 60s, this was still a pretty *outré* thing to do — especially when, back at school, I dictated the cast to fix those famous (and some less famous) names in their young minds. 'De Havilland... that's two words, and two "l"s.' This little excursion actually became a radio news item: at the cinema, I ran into the late Mary Hardy, Melbourne actress and comedienne, who perhaps then had a radio programme on which, to a no-doubt enthralled audience, she confided how she'd shared the screening with ninety twelve- or thirteen-year-olds in uniform. More formally and respectably, in 1975, the year before I left Trinity, I managed to introduce a whole strand of 'Film' into a Year 10 Communication class, which led me to take them to see (among others) *Chinatown* and *Murder on the Orient Express*, followed by some very serious discussions back at school.

I recall two other film-related episodes that I suspect don't do me much credit. At the end of the year a form-master was expected to organise some sort of outing for the boys in his form. In December 1964, while other staff were taking their classes sailing on Port Philip Bay or walking in the hills, I had neglected to make any such (unenticing) arrangements. At the last minute, I decided we would all go to see the film version of *Billy Liar* at Melbourne's Grosvenor Cinema, followed by tea at the adjacent Victoria Coffee Palace. We were all safely home by 5.30. This afternoon was the first sighting for many of these boys of Julie Christie, and if they're not grateful to me for that they certainly should be. That image of her swinging down the drab northern street is one of the imperishable moments of British cinema. I never supposed that thirty-odd years later I would meet her and that she would write the foreword to a book of mine. The other episode also came about as a result of self-protection (i.e., from the possibility of boredom). In order to avoid having to supervise one of those school trips where students are shown over factories, coalmines and the wonders of landscape, I devised five days in Sydney with a carefully hand-chosen group of six Year 12 students, and we simply went to the theatre and cinema all the time. We saw *Who's Afraid of Virginia Woolf*, and we all felt very cutting-edge when it later caused a scandal in Melbourne for its racy dialogue, and *Rattle of a Simple Man*, the last of the theatre offerings after which one boy said, 'This is the third prostitute's bedroom we've been in this week', but I can't now remember the other two plays that had led him to this observation. Our film-viewing on one day involved seeing Merle Oberon twice (a revival of *Wuthering Heights* and the 1964 load of old cobblers, *Of Love and Desire*). The mother of one of the boys chosen for this Sydney trip was heard to remark when it was mooted: 'It seems a long way just to go to the pictures,' but of course she was not taking into account the keenly critical discussions that followed all our viewing, was she? Quite recently my older daughter told me she'd been speaking to some acquaintances who'd never heard of Merle Oberon. Who *are* these people? I never was more shocked. Certainly no Trinity literature student of the 60s and early 70s would ever have displayed such ignorance.

As our children began to value the right things, they were of course initiated into the incomparable rewards of the cinema, and now the process is being repeated with grandchildren, some of whom have an access to popular culture I'd have sold my parents for. Back in December 1965, I took Duncan, then two and a half, to his first cinema (he'd slept more or less in the back seat of the car during *Birdman of Alcatraz* at the Drive-In, so you couldn't really count that) to see *Mary Poppins*. He liked this all right but not as much as the supporting cartoon which featured Donald Duck trying to fill a bucket with an over-powerful hose and to which Duncan responded with uncontrollable giggles that proved contagious in the cinema's largely youthful audience. In the 70s, I encouraged him to keep a chart of the films he saw with critical appraisals, but it must be said that the football, following which no written evaluations were required, came more naturally to his youthful self. However, there is a document, a large card sheet with columns headed FILM, STARS and COMMENT, on which his youthful views on *Blazing Saddles, The Sting, The Great MacArthy* and others are recorded. His critiques are stored safely in some place that neither of us can locate. I remember taking him and a rather nicely-behaved friend of his to *Blazing Saddles*, then being worried about the friend's reaction to its vulgarities which I tried to distract attention from by coughing or scrabbling for objects I'd deliberately dropped on the floor.

In the ensuing years, I saw an amazing number of children's films. The tastes of my daughters, Susannah and Sophie, ran more to animal-oriented pieces like *The Magic of Lassie* ('full of old people crying,' I heard Sophie tell her mother, and she meant the audience), *Flipper* (boy-and-dolphin), and *All Creatures Great and Small* (vets-and-anything): during these years adult film-going required serious negotiation (and baby-sitters). There were still memorable highlights, including those films that ushered a new, more radical spirit into American cinema: films like *Bonnie and Clyde, Easy Rider, Alice's Restaurant*, rougher, smarter than the classic Hollywood narratives film-goers of my generation had grown up on, and continental masters such as Bergman and Antonioni were peaking, with the likes of *Persona* and *Blow-Up* respectively. But it was expensive and the other claims on time and money kept increasing. Only television in those pre-video days enabled one to catch up on all the lost treasures of the 60s. And there seemed to be scarcely a break before the children of *my* children needed to be accompanied to appropriate multiplexes, but more of that later. Speaking of claims on one's limited funds reminds me of my effort to replenish these in early 1962 by becoming a competitor on Channel 7's *Coles £3000 Quiz*, taking American film 1940-1960 as my topic. If you didn't make it past the first three questions you were given three Embassy shirts (Coles' own brand) and thanked for coming along. Past question 3, you were assured of £24 and thanked for coming along. I made it to question 6 but flunked on 'What won the Oscar for Best Cartoon of 1944?' Gerie, who had been coaching me with the help of old film mags, had tried but failed to persuade me take cartoons more seriously in preparation for this opportunity of great wealth. She arrived at the studio after I'd been dismissed, bearing three new lampshades for the house we'd bought (I use the term 'bought' very loosely). These items had cost exactly £24. How could she have known that I'd just earnt exactly enough to pay for them?

Trinity Grammar School was the site of my first taking professional life seriously. The Headmaster, John Leppitt, was a humane, sometimes humanly irascible, man, given to large pronouncements. But — and this was a very major 'but' as far as I was concerned — if he felt you knew what you were doing he would offer very considerable support and give you *carte blanche* to get on with it. In my own case, he enabled me to build up English studies, to acquire for the School a respectable library to back these; he sanctioned numerous school excursions to the theatre and, sometimes, the cinema; he strongly favoured the production of plays and approved the expense that this often entailed; he allowed me to set up a one-act play festival; and he backed the introduction of what were then quite radical curriculum innovations. Looking back on it, I think Trinity was a school well suited to obsessives like me. The fact that there were other obsessives meant that there would be occasional clashes, but the chances were there, if you wanted them, to put your obsessions into useful practice. Thirty years on, it still seems to be a school of real character and achievement.

After eighteen months abroad in 1970-1971, I came back to Trinity, to which I must always be grateful for the opportunities it gave me. Not, perhaps, those of being Master-in-charge of 'winter tennis', a sport devised for those with no capacity for it, or any other game, or of Master-in-charge of Unpleasantness (not a formal title). This latter involved me in running and supervising detentions and rounding up offenders. One boy quibbled about my judgment and I replied firmly, '*I* am the master-in-charge of unpleasantness,' and he ventured to say, 'And very well suited to it you are sir.' An equivocal compliment at best I think. I am still seriously grateful for the unsought and rapid promotion in 1968 which found me as Acting Headmaster for a term, while John Leppitt was in hospital and the Senior Master, George Wood, was on study leave. This brief stint at such a dizzy height made quite forcibly clear to me that this was not the direction in which my ambitions — or, such as they were, my talents — lay. But more of that later. America intervened.

Chapter Seven
Fun in Acapulco (nothing to do with Elvis) ... or A man's gotta dream ...

I f it was not exactly my first thought when, in 1970, I won a Fulbright Award to teach for a year in an American college, it wasn't long after that I began to think of how I might get to meet Merle Oberon. But that is to race ahead somewhat. My first recollection of the announcement of the award is that of my three children, then seven, five and three respectively, bursting into collective tears. The last thing they wanted to do was to leave friends, schools, grandparents, the home and life they knew, to go adventuring they knew not where. A quick-thinking bribe saved the day. 'We'll take you to Disneyland,' we said, and the whole enterprise took on a new complexion. They were just sufficiently steeped in popular culture for the word to have a magic ring to it. Anyway, it worked and they didn't agonise again about leaving in three months' time for me to take up a position as lecturer at the Northwestern Michigan College, Traverse City. Only three-year-old Sophie, then a child of angelic goodness, suffered a relapse at the airport when she realised her grandparents weren't coming with us. Trinity Grammar School was happy enough to give me leave not just for the (northern) academic year but also to go on to England to do six months research into various educational developments. But this is not the place for an analysis of the radically shifting state of play in secondary-curriculum development in the latter half of the twentieth century.

We headed off via Sydney and Nadi, Fiji, to Hawaii, in company with three other Australian families on the Fulbright deal. Excitement was tempered by the fact that there was no hour when all three of our children were asleep together — they seemed to be working a shift system of wakefulness — but was given a lift by the luxuriance of Honolulu foliage and a kind of casual glamour about Waikiki and the place in general. Coming upon the Myrna Loy Gift Shop was the only connection with film, but it was good to think she had invested her earnings wisely. San Francisco, on the other hand, was full of resonances from such films as Hitchcock's *Vertigo* (1958), with Kim Novak leaping into the Bay and the Golden Gate Bridge in the background, and Peter Yates's *Bullitt* (1968), with Steve McQueen's dizzying chase scenes up and down those improbable urban hills, not to speak of the exuberant tones of Jeannette MacDonald in *San Francisco* (1936) surmounting the challenge of the 1906 earthquake, and Judy Garland extolling the beauties of 'the only bridge that's a real gone bridge, … the bridge across the bay.' And crossing the bridge we saw to the east Alcatraz where Burt Lancaster had done his stuff as 'Birdman'. You could buy postcards of Alcatraz with the legend 'Wish you were here'. Disneyland, in turn, did the trick as far as our kids were concerned, and was in fact a marvel of inventiveness and attention to detail. Anticipating that idiotic film franchise by three decades, we undertook the 'Pirates of the Caribbean' tour — so much quicker, and really more exciting, than Johnny Depp and co. The flight to Washington took us over landscapes that seemed to come straight from John Ford westerns. Or do I have that the wrong way around? Whichever, almost everything we saw in our first weeks in America reminded me of where I'd first had any idea of what it was: I'd have sworn that was Joan Blondell waiting table in Washington or that William Demarest was the doorman at our hotel.

Traverse City was not then, and probably is still not, a centre of film culture. It was essentially a college town (of about 25,000 people), idyllically set on the shores of Lake Michigan and surrounded by woods that forever seemed to be encroaching on the town. Snow fell first on 21 November, by chance the night of the College's progressive dinner, which we, unprepared, sat through soaked to the ankles, and last fell on 19 May (admittedly this was freakish). We were told by neighbours that 'It's man against nature up here, and man doesn't always win', a not wholly cheery proposition for visitors. It *was* a demanding climate to live in, but, once adjusted to, Traverse City was also serenely beautiful in all seasons: lush in spring and summer, ablaze in the northern manner in autumn, and in winter even its most commonplace streets, like the one we lived on, took on a touch of white poetry. Looking back, I'm amazed though that I ever had the nerve to drive off in blizzards as we sometimes did, or that Gerie was compliant about this, especially in our ancient Ford Galaxy which provided the College's automotive section with its practical work component for most of the academic year, and, miraculously, seized up only once — on a highway outside Chilicothe, Ohio, on a wintry Sunday afternoon. Other Fulbright visitors ended up in larger metropolises, like New York in one case, but with three small children we were lucky to have drawn the more benign Traverse City, and were treated with immense kindness and hospitality.

American colleagues were apt to be surprised at anyone as exotic as an Australian having a passion for their ancient movies, and this was a time when Hollywood was beginning to be taken seriously by film scholars, not just audiences. It transpired that Veronica Lake, long remembered for her 'peekaboo bang', had been married (for her, one of several occasions) in Traverse City, the very Michigan town in which we'd fetched up. Colleagues were also surprised that I could be bothered going to the Cherry County Playhouse to see a play called *Best of Friends*, the final in the theatre's summer season. Most of the plays starred current or slightly *passé* television favourites, such as Imogene Coca or Bob (*Hogan's Heroes*) Crane, who were of little interest to me, but *Best of Friends* co-starred Macdonald Carey and Barbara Britton, who had both had Hollywood careers in the 40s and 50s. They were of course well past the days of the minor stardom they had once enjoyed, but I remembered them fondly for some of their Paramount films: laconic Carey in *The Streets of Laredo*, as a bandit, or as Nick Caraway in *The Great Gatsby*; and Britton had been 'deeply moving' as a nun helping Ray Milland to escape from occupied France in *Till We Meet Again*. By dint of sending a possibly impertinent letter,

I actually got to meet Britton, who was a sweet woman, happy to reminisce about her studio days in Hollywood, and about her 1952 role in the first 3D feature film, the supremely idiotic *Bwana Devil*, into which we'd been lured by the promise of 'A lover in your arms! A lion in your lap!' I kept hoping film actors would cross my path in the US but they didn't, though people working in shops and banks and schools all could have been there by courtesy of Central Casting. We had to pay serious money to see Alexis Smith, elegant 'other woman' of Warner Bros. dramas, in Stephen Sondheim's great musical, *Follies*, on Broadway. This was, however, money very well spent, because not only was long-legged Smith brilliantly glamorous and still sexily alluring but the cast also included other Hollywood names, dancer Gene Nelson, veteran of Warners' musicals, and Yvonne De Carlo. The latter, 'the most beautiful girl in the world', as she had been modestly hyped in the 40s, appropriately enough stopped the show by singing 'I'm still here', as so, patently, she was. And for connoisseurs of Hollywood trivia, in support were Arnold Moss, a sinister figure in any number of thrillers and melodramas since playing an Egyptian police chief on Merle's trail in *Temptation* (1946), and Fifi D'Orsay, once touted as Hollywood's 'French Bombshell', and here playing 'Solange La Fitte'. The name tells all. *Follies* was a treat enough in itself, but the presence of these five old-time movie alumni was a bonus indeed for me.

Back in Traverse City, there was one cinema, which showed contemporary American films such as *Joe* (held to be controversial at the time and unheard of in the decades since) and *Diary of a Mad Housewife* (less controversial, but still unheard of since), but not much else. The College ran seasons of art house films where I was pleased to see again Antonioni's *Blow-Up* and, for the first time, such oddities as Joseph Strick's brave adaptation of Joyce's *Ulysses* and Robert Enrico's beautiful version of Ambrose Bierce's superb short story, *The Occurrence at Owl Creek Bridge*. My main viewing, though, was on TV, and cable television, unknown in Australia in 1970-1971, yielded choice pickings, of both old classics and a lot of

1960s titles early fatherhood had prevented me from seeing at the time. The former included the likes of *42nd Street, Laura* and *The Searchers*, archetypal Warners' musical, *noir* thriller and western respectively; while the latter included Buzz Kulik's smart thriller *Warning Shot*, with such seniors as Lilian Gish and Walter Pidgeon fleshing out support for TV hero David Janssen, Joseph Losey's bizarre *Secret Ceremony*, with Elizabeth Taylor involved in some very strange goings-on, and Martin Ritt's tough western, *Hombre*, with Paul Newman as the hombre of the title. Both golden old'uns and missed sixties are unmemorably recorded in my diaries of the time. I particularly recall one of the midday screenings on a Wednesday (which I often watched because of having no classes) in late October in which the presenter was interviewing a witch during a break in the film. 'I guess this is a busy time of the year for you,' she said straight-faced to the witch, Hallowe'en hovering as it was. 'Oh, yes,' she agreed, equally straight-faced, so that you expected her to start mixing lethal potions before your eyes. All this was in the interests of securing our attention for a deeply ridiculous shocker called *The House That Would Not Die*, involving Barbara Stanwyck and Richard Egan, and of which I wrote, 'Like all feature films made for TV, this has terrible sets, sparse casts, thin characterisation and no sense of place'. A bit severe perhaps, but probably near the truth as things were then. Nevertheless, one had to be grateful to cable TV for a chance to see — again or for the first time — titles such as those listed above.

A Trinity Grammar student had passed on to me an article from *Life* magazine in 1967 about Merle Oberon's idling her life away in Acapulco, in a house called 'El Ghalal' ('from an ancient Mexican-Indian phrase meaning "to love"'), with bouts of entertaining visiting royalty. I thoughtfully filed this piece, with its provocative title, 'In a Swinging Resort the Star Is Merle Oberon' (3 April 1967). When I knew we were going to America, I wrote to her at 'El Ghalal', suggesting that she and I should take advantage of our being in the same continent for once to meet. To my surprise and huge gratification, shortly after arriving in Michigan, I had a reply saying she'd 'be delighted to meet' me and giving phone numbers and addresses. Accordingly, our Christmas holiday plans took us south, first to Texas, from which it seemed to me it would be but the work of an hour to fly the border to Mexico. After an exchange of letters, one of which from her charmingly included my wife and children in the invitation, I finally secured these latter in a motel room in San Antonio and made my way south of the border. This jaunt was finally conducted alone because my wife (who, as I said earlier, looked like Merle when we were married) generously, if sardonically, felt 'A man's gotta dream' and, less generously but more pragmatically, looking at our kids, decided they were only moderately well-behaved and would probably knock over a valuable artefact or catch a disease. Our Traverse City travel agent was mystified as to why I'd be going to Acapulco alone while the others stayed in San Antonio, but I didn't clarify this for her, though she gave me many opportunities to do so.

In fact, my diary records how gloomy I felt at leaving nearest and dearest behind as I flew first to Mexico City, then to Acapulco airport where a maniacal driver to my relief and surprise delivered me to the Auto Ritz Hotel. After a fitful night's sleep and a cautious breakfast, having in mind all those stories of instant dysentery lying in wait for unwary travellers in Mexico and not wanting to mar the day ahead, I was relieved when Merle's chauffeur arrived at 10.30 to transport me to the House of Love. Over precipitous and lumpy roads we arrived at the Pagliai mansion (Merle was then married to Italian industrialist Bruno Pagliai), to be met at the door by the lady herself. After nearly a quarter-century of helpless adoration, it seemed scarcely possible, but there she was, looking fabulous in, my diary says, pink slacks and shirt, with long dark hair hanging loose, the face a thing of olivine perfection and the figure as gracefully sculpted as ever. She escorted me through the house, via her bedroom where I observed her bedside reading to be Nicholas Montserrat's *The Nylon Pirates*, perhaps not indicative of the very highest literary tastes, to sit beside the pool, shaded with banana trees and palms, and to absorb the stunning vista of the bay — and the even more stunning vista of Merle on her chaise longue. She had been having trouble with architects (the house was put up for sale shortly afterwards), servants (so hard to get decent staff in Mexico) and health. She'd been diagnosed by her doctor over the phone as having hepatitis, and, while there was no one I'd rather have caught it from, I was hoping it wasn't contagious. The phone rang several times in the first hour of my visit, including one from her brother-in-law who apparently recommended another doctor, but Merle said firmly, 'No, he's the one who prescribes pills that kill people.' I began to feel I should leave in case she was getting tired, but she insisted she wasn't and I stayed nearly three hours, during which some of those unsatisfactory servants plied us with cool drinks. She offered lunch but this seemed too much for someone who was meant to be unwell.

I'm glad I hadn't read some of the stories about her, or Charles Higham and Roy Moseley's 1983 biography, *Merle*, before the visit: they certainly would have punctured my more or less innocent vision of this miraculous beauty. They might also have lessened my wife's willingness to send me off alone on this pilgrimage. As it was, I simply sat there drinking in the beauty — and enjoying the talk. She was relaxed, kind, well-informed and had lots of firm opinions; she liked talking about her films and those of others and was neither the conventional charmer nor the bitchy socialite the gossip columns sometimes suggested. She was planning to visit London later in 1971 (this didn't happen) and insisted I must bring Gerie and the kids to meet her there. Very kindly she sent Gerie a pair of Mexican pottery birds and for the kids some nicely made Mexican clothes her children had grown out of. It was not her fault that my son didn't wear embroidered blouses or that my daughters were planning to be boys when they grew up and wouldn't wear the hand-wrought dresses. She talked freely of all sorts of film-famous names: Rita Hayworth, 'Larry' Olivier, Noël Coward, Miriam Hopkins — 'all technique, no feeling', Maurice Chevalier, Harry Cohn, Spencer Tracy (he'd told her the Oscars meant nothing when she didn't get one for *Wuthering Heights*), Greer Garson, William Wyler, etc, etc. She probably had a higher opinion of *A Song to Remember* than most critics would feel able to share, but who cared about historical verisimilitude when Merle was on screen? And she warded off potential criticism (as if I were about to offer any!) by praising Columbia's ogre-boss, Harry Cohn, for buying up a Polish film about Chopin just so that he could reproduce one scene. This scene was the one in which Chopin (Cornel Wilde) plays to a distinguished audience in the dark, and everyone thinks it must be Liszt. Gardeners and other menials cease their chores to whisper, 'Ssh! Liszt!', then Merle comes in bearing a candelabra to reveal that the performance the audience has been applauding is by Chopin playing his own composition. She also talked about her adopted children, Bruno and Francesca, and about American life and manners — most of her views on the latter would not have been helpful to the national image. When I asked if I could take some photos of her, she said yes, and added that 'Prince Philip had been there only a week or so earlier with such a cunning little camera, no bigger than your finger'. My resulting photos are only a little blurred, are in fact as good as you could expect from a shaking hand.

I mentioned the gossip columns before. In our first few months in America, Merle was constantly being referred to in a column as a rule simply under the by-line of 'Suzy', occasionally signed off as 'Suzy Knickerbocker' (could that have been her real name?). We would see this in the *Detroit Free Press*, but I think it was syndicated more widely, and always bore an image of the lethal-looking Suzy. She claimed to have been to 'an awful lot of parties and a lot of awful parties', but, under the headline of 'That Merle Always Thinks of Everything' (8 December 1970), she enthused about the bash Merle had organised to celebrate the inauguration of the new President of Mexico. And to think that only two weeks later she was offering me lunch and not looking at all exhausted, in spite of suspected hepatitis. Well, while I was there, I urged her to get back to the movies which so sorely needed her in grungy 1970, and I strongly recommended that she enlist the support of George Cukor to direct and Henry Fonda to co-star with her in a screen version of Henry James's *The Ambassadors*. She wasn't familiar with this subtle and glittering work, but I assured her she was born to play Madame de Vionnet who so effortlessly captivates men across a wide age-spectrum. On return to Traverse City, I sent her a copy (she wrote thanking me for 'the Henry James book'). She was curiously absent from the gossip columns over the next few months and I pointed this out to my wife who simply, if perhaps not wholly kindly, said, 'Don't be silly, she's at home with a tutor trying to read *The Ambassadors.*' The other roles I wanted her to play were the title role in a version of Angus Wilson's *The Middle Age of Mrs Eliot*, though I didn't quite like to name it in case it seemed rude in the face of her ageless beauty, and Jocasta in *Oedipus Rex*. I mean, how many women are old enough to be your mother but ravishing enough to make you want to marry them? In the event, of course, she followed none of my suggestions but made an ill-fated comeback in *Interval* in 1973, divorced her industrialist husband, and married her co-star, Robert Wolders, who as Gerie pointed out to me, again not all that kindly, 'is younger than you are.' Only very recently have I been able to buy a copy of *Interval* (never screened in Australia). It is not, I have to say, much of a film but Merle looks sumptuous in and out of a lavishly designed wardrobe. And romps on the beach with Wolders — in a bikini!

Merle has been dead now for nearly thirty years, and I've met quite a number of film stars since, several of them quite gorgeously beautiful, but I suppose that having been caught young by Merle's dark charms helps account for the fact that none has ever dislodged her image from my mind. On the day she died, my son was working at his desk, or so he said, with the radio on, and kept giving us reports of the latest speculation on her age. It seems certain now that she was born, in India, in 1911, not Tasmania as she was still claiming when I met her in December 1970. She was then fifty-nine, or, as she would have preferred to put it, fifty-two: whichever, she didn't look a day over thirty-five. Writing, as I did, an obituary for her in the Melbourne journal *Cinema Papers* (Feb-March, 1980) seemed like a sad privilege. It was worth taking up a Fulbright for the chance to meet her — and to feel my youthful infatuation had been vindicated.

I still feel this every time I re-see, say, *Lydia* or *Dark Angel*, and, sensing the need for another viewing of *A Song to Remember* coming on, I recently acquired and watched a DVD. I can only say my youthful judgment was spot on. A domestic memory of the early 1970s: we had two pet sheep grazing in our back yard, the first of whom was unimaginatively named Lambsy, but I stipulated that we could only have a second if it was called Merle, so it was. Mind you the names of the innumerable household pets of this period were inclined to be idiosyncratic: there were two terrapins called Timothy and Jimothy and two nasty budgerigars called Hopefully and Substantive, after my two least favourite words at the time. But I digress ...

The rest of the time in America was taken up with teaching, keeping the kids happy, and generally doing whatever came our way. We all hired skates when the town froze over one of the sports ovals, and I spent a good deal of time horizontal while Gerie showed Sonja Henie potential and even the children evinced some skill. I still recall Gerie standing over my prone form and uttering the very Australian but not wholly sympathetic words: 'Come a gutser didn' ya.' I acquired college credits for cross-country skiing on Saturdays but was unable to set these against the Melbourne University MA thesis I was writing while we were away. My son and I regularly went to the College basketball matches at which the highlight was apt to be the performance of the cheer-leaders at half-time. Fortunately, I was saved from a weekend's camping in the woods with him and his cub-scout troop by his cub mistress's coming down with scarlet fever at the crucial time. I was very sorry for her of course. We were also invited to slide down a snowy slope by moonlight sitting in aluminium (called aluminum in the US) saucers when a merciful thaw saved us. We had Thanksgiving holiday in New York, ferried to the Statue of Liberty, saw the big parade and the Rockettes at Radio City Music Hall at the first screening of *Scrooge*. But enough of this: I was there to work and did; there was a strong element of good-will mission about it, so that we did what we were asked and enjoyed a great deal of it.

In the following six months in London, from July 1971, we realised how different being there with three small children was from how it had been in our irresponsible early twenties. For instance, I counted at one point and found I'd been in twenty-seven different parks for play purposes, as opposed to a sophisticated ramble on Hampstead Heath twelve years ago. In spite of these infant demands on my time, I'm surprised to find that I did manage to see seventy plays or films between 7 July and 13 January. Not only *see*, but also write about them at remarkable length. By this time, I expect I must acknowledge that writing about film (and theatre while in England) had become a compulsive activity. There are pages of diary accounts of, say, Frank Lloyd's film version of Coward's *Cavalcade*, at the National Film Theatre, Christopher Miles's intelligent and sensitive adaptation of Lawrence's *The Virgin and the Gypsy*, Robert Mulligan's similarly intelligent and sensitive *Summer of '42*, about coming-of-age on Long Island, and Joseph Losey's eloquent version of L.P. Hartley's *The Go-Between*, among many others squeezed in among park visits. This rate of viewing and writing was sustained throughout the rest of 1971, so, in spite of getting on with educational researches for Trinity Grammar School and doing duty in parks and other child-oriented venues, I can't really have been badly deprived. I remember one day taking son Duncan on a bus tour of London (as many buses as you could fit in for a small daily fee) and asking him which film title this reminded him of, expecting no more than a reference to the moronic *On the Buses* currently screening on TV, and being impressed with his reply — *Long Day's Journey Into Night*. So the training hadn't been entirely wasted.

There was a lot of travelling during these six months, most of it in a shonky second-hand Volkswagen 'beetle' (which broke down on a Swiss autoroute) and none of it really relevant here. I was supposed to be doing useful things for Trinity, and up to a point I did. One journey took us to the south-west of England in a drear November, and, returning from Cornwall to our lodgings in Totnes one gloomy late afternoon, I tried bribing the children into silent observation with a penny for every Dartmoor pony they saw. One quick look out the car's windows assured them that there were none to be seen and they resumed bickering immediately. My next strategy was to offer a shilling for the first escaped convict they could identify (perhaps recalling the apparition of Magwitch on the marshes in David Lean's *Great Expectations*, 1946). Shortly after this idea was launched, we were stopped by a roadblock and were told that one was 'out'. This added immensely to the kids' excitement and to my apprehension, especially when Duncan wound down his window and yelled to the police who'd just let us through: 'He's in the boot.' I expect five people in a 'beetle' made it seem unlikely to the cops, because they didn't pursue us. Next day, at Taunton, we heard that the escapee had been 'inside' for armed robbery, which made me even gladder not to have sighted him. After such dramas, life back in Australia in January 1972 must have seemed very calm by comparison, but changes were looming for me, and in the direction I wanted to go.

There were two film-related occasions in London dutifully recorded in the diaries. One was a personal appearance at the National Film Theatre of Olivia De Havilland. Before she came in, the audience was treated to a montage of some of her more famous roles, including *A Midsummer Night's Dream* and, in ravishing colour (I mean *she* looked ravishing) in *The Adventures of Robin Hood*. Following these rewarding glimpses of the eighteen- and twenty-year-old De Havilland, the lady herself — trim of figure, blonde of hair and unlined of face — entered, scarcely looking thirty-five years older. She either knew we'd think that or perhaps she just had a healthy ego. In any event, she was articulate, amusing and intelligent, and it was easy to sense the discipline and purpose that had made her so reliably interesting an actress and such a thorn in the flesh to Warner Bros. She was generous and astute about the likes of William Wyler, Bette Davis and the dire-sounding Errol Flynn, and she deserved the ovation she got from the packed audience. There was a packed audience, too, for Gladys Cooper's Memorial Service, held on her birthday, 18 December 1971. I snuck in at the back, with genial permission of her son-in-law Robert Morley, who seemed to be welcoming people at the door of St Paul's

Covent Garden. I went partly because I'd admired her as an actress — in films she was one of those character players who were always the object of my special attention, perhaps because there seemed to be a special kind of concentration about the way they made their presences felt in often brief scenes, whereas stars could take their time. Gladys Cooper was one who stood in numerous Hollywood films, supposedly set in England, for a reality of Britishness that the stars were sometimes struggling to suggest. My other reason for going was that I thought there might be glimpses of other actors fondly regarded for their film work — and indeed there were. Not just Morley who did an eloquent and witty address, or Stanley Holloway who read from Bunyan (the 'To be a pilgrim' episode), or Celia Johnson who gave a heartfelt reading of Shakespeare's Sonnet CXVI, though that was a good start. As well, though, there were the likes of John Gielgud, Joyce Grenfell, Joan Greenwood, Paul Scofield, Dinah Sheridan, Roland Culver, Moira Lister and, very old and moving, Sybil Thorndike, booming on the steps later: 'Lovely party. How Gladys would have loved it.' There were lots of anecdotes circulating about Cooper at this time. My favourite (it may have been part of Morley's eulogy) had her arriving at a hotel in Chicago and trying to book a room, only to be told there were none available because 'General Motors is holding a conference.' Her reply was 'The General is a friend of mine. He will be very happy for me to have a room.'

The main legacy of this time away is that I was now writing about films and plays at a length and from an analytical point of view that I hadn't previously aspired to. The fact that no one but myself was reading what I wrote didn't matter. I was beginning to find the way that I wanted to write. It was no longer a matter of a careful plod through plot and performance, with wise summarising opinions, but of trying to give a sense of the wholeness of the experience, to understand what the filmmaker (or playwright/producer) was up to, and how such intentions were articulated through the strategies of cinematic story-telling. That sounds a bit solemn, but the challenge was to be serious while at the same time to avoid being solemn.

Chapter Eight
Combining business and pleasure

Whereas loving film so much was in my youth pretty much a guilty pleasure (only foreign films were really respectable), it has been good to live long enough to see film as not merely a poor man's option but for it to have become a wildly popular discipline of study. Soon, it will probably be compulsory. No longer do you need to sneak it surreptitiously into English courses. At tertiary level, you are almost encouraged to slip the word 'film' into the title of an English Department subject offering in the sure hope of its attracting a substantial intake of students ('Shakespeare and Film', 'Novel into Film', etc). For a while they were perhaps drawn by the idea of film as an entertainment (how could watching a film possibly be work?), but, from the mid 1970s on, a lot of very serious film theory would quickly disabuse them of this idea.

Towards the mid 1970s I decided I wanted to try for a position in tertiary education. It was not a matter of being unhappy at Trinity Grammar, but of not wanting to go on doing the same thing for the rest of my career. Even that word 'career' points, I suppose, to the inevitable growing seriousness of purpose I needed to assume. I'd been appointed Senior Master at the end of 1975, and this position — second to the headmaster — involved me in more administration than I either cared for or could efficiently do. Further, it became apparent to me that if I stayed in this secondary system I'd probably end up applying for a headship, and some desperate school might just have been careless enough in its selection procedures to offer me one. I knew this would be in neither the school's nor my potential best interests, and I wasn't just guessing about this. In 1968 when the then-senior master was on study leave and the headmaster had to go to hospital for surgery, I had very accelerated promotion for a school term in which I was acting headmaster. 'Acting' was the key word. It didn't come naturally to me, and, though some excuse might have been made for me on the grounds of my comparative youth (i.e., early thirties), I couldn't help feeling that dealing with the demands of staff, students, parents and council took more time than I was happy to give. What I liked was teaching, literature as it was at this time, and I didn't have the patience or the flair for ensuring those four important groups were getting their just deserts — or seeing eye to eye with each other. I've seen other people do this job with tact and creative skills, but have always been glad of that late-sixties sampling of the top job which convinced me that it was not the one for me.

During my time at Trinity, after completing the MA preliminary requirements, I'd had some experience of university tutoring (1968-1969), and found this very congenial. At the University of Melbourne I'd done a couple of years with Rhetoric students and I don't remember much of this obscure branch of the English Department, except that it involved some rigorous, detailed reading and analysis of the likes of Jonathan Swift and Samuel Johnson. However, the regular Year 2 English (the big names of 19th and 20th centuries from Jane Austen to James Joyce) was more in my line, and I enjoyed the stimulus of these late-afternoon classes peopled largely by 'mature-age' students. They needed to be enjoyable, coming, as they did for me, after a full day at Trinity. This pattern was repeated in a two-year stint (1972-1973) in the La Trobe University English Department, and by this time I was sure that I wanted to move into tertiary teaching. Fortunately for me, this was also a time when such opportunities were opening up, unlike the bleak present when departments skimp, with staff and resources at low ebb.

Having finished my MA (an uninspiring tract on aspects of Australian fiction), I began to apply for positions in tertiary education and I became adept at writing applications, making the most of minimal publication history and minimising deficiencies. The result was that in 1976 I was appointed Head of the Department of English and Community Languages at the Frankston State College of Victoria, where despite some undeniably taxing times I relished the change in atmosphere from that of school, where one's day was inevitably controlled by bells. I even grew to enjoy travelling on what were then Victorian Railways' 'red rattlers' and became almost certainly one of the best-read people in the State College system as a result. Tiresomely disciplined as I was/am, I would read the newspaper from Caulfield to Moorabbin, and from there to Frankston (and all the way back in the late afternoon) *Anna Karenina* or other magisterial works that required a lot of concentrated attention. Perhaps the most enjoyable aspect of this job was that of devising and teaching courses in (mainly Australian) literature, as part of the teacher-training courses offered at the College, and eventually I was also able to offer courses in film to yet other mature-age students who returned to take the Bachelor of Education courses available in the evenings. Like most courses on film, these always attracted large numbers of enthusiastic students happy to discuss anything from *Battleship Potemkin* (has there ever been a film course on which it does not figure?) to *Psycho*. The emphasis at Frankston was very properly on the primary teacher-training aspects of the programmes: I hadn't the background to contribute much to this, so that I needed to develop the sorts of courses I've mentioned. And to accept the fact that, to most of my students, however much they may have enjoyed these, they were not of first importance to them. As well, I was expected to do a good deal of administrative work and to spend a lot of time at meetings, concealing as best I could my distaste for these occupations. I suppose it's unreasonable to expect that all of one's working life will be pure pleasure, but in the ensuing decades I must say I found it to be nearly so.

There is always pressure on academics to publish and, after wringing my MA thesis dry like an old sponge, I began to write on other literary matters, including a 1978 article on that unsung heroine of the 20th-century novel, Ivy Compton-Burnett, and a small book on Martin Boyd's 'Langton novels' in 1980, and, at greater length than ever before, I began writing on film, and have done so compulsively ever since. The Melbourne-based film journal, *Cinema Papers*, was thriving in the 1970s, and, through the intervention of Tom Ryan, later film reviewer for the *Sunday Age*, and whom I first heard giving a lecture on my director-idol John Ford, I became one of *Cinema Papers*' regular reviewers. Under the editorship of Scott Murray and Peter Beilby, *Cinema Papers* flourished at the time of the revival of Australian filmmaking in the 70s. Most of the films I was asked to review were Australian, and they included some key titles of the period: *The Getting of Wisdom*, *The Chant of Jimmie Blacksmith*, *My Brilliant Career* and *The Mango Tree*. What these films all had in common — apart from their focus on young people, rites of passage and a specific concern with projecting aspects of the national character — was that they were all adaptations of popular or classic Australian novels. There were other — in hindsight perhaps livelier — films being made in Australia then, films such as *Sunday Too Far Away*, that important study of masculinity in peculiarly Australian conditions; or the genre pieces *Money Movers* or *Mad Max*; or the social realist studies of urban life *The FJ Holden* or *Mouth to Mouth*. The adaptations, though, were, arguably, the ones that established the revival as a film wave to be reckoned with at the time.

With a teaching and research interest in the adaptation phenomenon, I put it to a publisher that a book about Australian films derived from Australian novels might be a goer, and, with the cooperation of *Cinema Papers*, Heinemann Publishers Australia agreed to take on *Words and Images: Australian Novels into Film* (1983). At this stage, as I was straddling the academic worlds of literature and film, this was an appropriate move for me, though, despite the colon in the title so essential to academic publishing, and despite the fact that it sold well, it was probably seen as too lacking in an essential theoretical framework. (This also means that it was accessible to large numbers of non-specialists who wouldn't have thanked me for references to structuralism or Derrida.) As well, adaptation study, certainly then and in some quarters possibly still today, was seen as a bit lightweight by committed literary scholars and a bit fuddy-duddy by the ferocious new breed of film academics. However, having the comfort of a permanent position meant that I needed not to be in awe of either of these groups and in a few years took myself to the University of East Anglia to begin study towards a PhD thesis on adaptation of novels into film.

Tertiary education suited me, with its emphasis on teaching and research, though there was still enough administration to test my meagre capacities in this direction, especially when I was appointed Head of the Arts Division at Frankston. This was one of those moves — there'd be many more of them in the next twenty years — designed to economise on staff and resources. The admin load became more than enough as time went on and the federal government embarked on a series of traumatic amalgamations of tertiary institutions. Traumatic, that is, for the staff involved, and a great deal of distress was caused to individuals in the interests of what were euphemistically called 'economies of scale', which really meant cutting everything to the bone and creating redundancies. As it happened, I was one of the lucky ones. Though I was 'amalgamated' twice in ten years, the result was that after each I was shorn of all manner of importance and self-importance and ended up being paid for doing exactly what I liked best: teaching, research and writing, at Monash University. The actual amalgamation procedures and periods, however, were about as much fun as heart surgery, and some people sadly never found rewarding work again. In nearly ten years at Chisholm Institute of Technology after the first shotgun academic marriage, I was free to develop subjects in literature and to introduce a whole course in film, and my writing found outlets both in reviewing and in more sustained pieces, as well as the books mentioned earlier. The film courses would expand to include studies of Australian and British cinemas, of adaptation from literature to film, and of film and ideology. It was particularly rewarding to see how absorbed students could become in the study of the British filmmaking period from just before World War 2 to the end of the British 'new wave', roughly 1965, from, as it were, *The Stars Look Down* to *This Sporting Life*. American films came naturally to them, but some found a whole new interest in a cinema they knew almost nothing of and in a period finished well before they were born. What I needed now were some qualifications in film studies, though there was plenty of incidence, both at home and abroad, of interested people moving into the area and educating themselves in it.

I was advised to embark on PhD study and, because there was no one in Australia in a position to supervise the thesis I wanted to undertake, I applied for enrolment at the University of East Anglia, Norwich. I also wanted to be supervised by Charles Barr who, like me, had had a background in literature. He was then one of the pioneers of film study in England, having written a definitive study of Ealing Studios, and is now one of its most revered names. This Norwich interlude was a demanding and stimulating time: demanding because it meant leaving family behind for the nine months of the northern academic year (with a month's break in January when Gerie came over) but certainly stimulating because of the way it made me focus on film study and writing. As well as supervising my thesis, Charles, whose *Ealing Studios* (1977, and since revised and reprinted twice) was a magisterial study of the ethos of one of Britain's most famous production units, also involved me in doing lectures on film adaptations and in writing a chapter on them for a book he was editing on British cinema, called *All Our Yesterdays: 90 Years of British Cinema* (1986). In these ways, the two main strands to my future critical writing were emerging, and over the next twenty years, along with a great deal of reviewing and editing, I seemed to be working incessantly on either adaptation or British cinema. When I say work, it seems a curious term to apply to activities so wholly enjoyable, and the fact that academics are *meant* to be researching and writing also meant that I never needed to feel guilty about this, despite that comment of my wife's suggesting that I'd made my hobbies my work so as always to look busy. Such a cynical perception.

The thesis was finally finished and accepted and found an afterlife in a few articles in the US journal *Literature/Film Quarterly*, and in a book called *Novel to Film:*[NB colon again] *An Introduction to the Theory of Adaptation*, published by OUP's Clarendon Press in 1996. Such a catchy title and everything in it is footnoted within an inch of its life, every formulation carefully qualified. However, though nothing would induce me to read it again, I am happy to say that it goes on selling and was gratified to find at a conference in Bath in 1999 that it has been prescribed in India, Spain and — most pleasing of all — Malta. For all I know, it is now required reading in Tibet and Ecuador. The interest in adaptation has recently led me to read *Sin City*, my first graphic fiction (such work is now big in adaptation), since growing up with the comic-strip adventures of *Mandrake*, in my mother's *Women's Weekly*, where I also read my first film criticism. I quite early decided that, while fidelity may be highly desirable for marriage or relationships generally, in the matter of adaptations playing around yielded more exciting results. While devotees of Jane Austen, for example, tend not to be happy with the slightest narrative or character diversion, as they see it, from the sacred originals, and thus admire the 1995 television miniseries' deferential plod through *Pride and Prejudice*, I greatly prefer Joe Wright's social-realist take on the 'truth universally acknowledged'. For once, it looked as if the Bennets' farm was a reality, rather than just a word.

In Australia, it was still the local cinema that attracted most of the critical writing about film. For me, it was a fortunate coincidence that, just as I was hitting my writing stride, Australian cinema was burgeoning. From the mid seventies, there had been a remarkable upsurge of filmmaking here, of a kind people of my age could scarcely credit. I grew up almost never seeing Australian films, and could count the titles seen before 1970 on the fingers of both hands, possibly even allowing for damage to one. There had been a few British- and US-backed films in the preceding decades, and they have their place in the history of those meagre years of filmmaking in Australia. I can remember giving a hostile review in *Film Bulletin* to the 20th Century-Fox 'western', *Kangaroo* (1952), set in South Australia, with Hollywood stars (Maureen O'Hara and Peter Lawford) and locals performing minor functions. It was typical of US films that used Australia as an exotic backdrop for conventional stories that might have been set anywhere. Britain, especially Ealing Studios, was more conscientious in seeking out stories with genuinely Australian interest, such as *The Overlanders* (1946) and *Eureka Stockade* (1949). Ealing in fact sought a continuing interest in filming in Australia and the studio's last film, *The Siege of Pinchgut* (1959), was shot in Sydney Harbour. It is against this sort of background that the excitement of the feature-film revival of the 1970s, and the writing it attracted, has to be seen. The writing had, of course, been correspondingly meagre until this efflorescence of the 70s.

The Australian film-writing community was a small and somewhat jealously guarded preserve in the eighties, and, despite some comforting critical appraisals here, the books I then published on aspects of Australian cinema — *Words and Images* and *Australian Cinema 1970-1985* (1986) — were generally better received critically overseas than locally. There were suggestions that people who came from English departments were less likely to be trusted on matters of film than those from — oh, practically any other. There was something to be said for this prejudice: academics from English departments were/are more ready to offer critical judgments about film without having any background in the ways that film goes about making its meanings than academics trained in film are about literary matters. The ways in which, say, subtlety or complexity or pathos is achieved in the audio-visual moving images of film are different from those deriving from words printed in straight lines on a page. Nothing could stop *Words and Images* from selling, though, perhaps because there was no competitor in the field, but apart from, say, Joel Greenberg's laudatory review in the *Sydney Morning Herald*, most of the critiques of *Australian Cinema 1970-1985* seemed to want a different book, one that played down the mainstream, for instance, and played up the less-seen subversive underbelly (*Shirley Thompson v. the Aliens*, rather than *Picnic at Hanging Rock*, for instance). Also, the book had been commissioned by the British firm of Secker & Warburg, though it was bought and imprinted by Heinemann Australia and Columbia University Press, USA, and this probably did not endear it locally. It also accounts in part for its attempt to concentrate on those films whose titles may have meant something — internationally. Even locally, though, I'd have thought it peculiar to focus on films which had been seen only by small, more specialised audiences. All this may just sound defensively like self-justification, but I was gratified that Philip French, London's leading film critic then and now, liked it enough to seek me out for an interview about Australian film when he was in the country in 1988. I know there are people who say they never read reviews of their own work, whether films or books, but I'm not sure that I believe them. I *do* read reviews of my books, and try to be very mature about those imperceptive critics who presume to find fault with them.

One pleasing result of these early books was an invitation to teach a semester course on Australian cinema at Klagenfurt University, Austria. The invitation at least was pleasing and so was much of the sojourn there, but the rub was that the semester course was to be taught in a fortnight, at the rate of four hours each day. The students were very earnest and their English was impressive when, say, they were giving papers, but they weren't really confident enough in it for the give-and-take of discussion. As a result I spent most of the four hours talking (they were expected to see the films in advance, so that there wasn't the respite of a screening), and each afternoon I would stagger ashen-faced to a downtown café to meet Gerie for *Kaffee und Kuchen*, an all-but broken man. Franz Kuna who arranged the visit went on to write widely on Australian film. He also took us on a jaunt into Slovenia without having checked whether we had visas. We didn't so he hid our passports under his own, hoping we wouldn't be arrested. We hoped this too and were not encouraged by his wife's cheery accounts of how illegal immigrants were housed and treated in this recently war-torn country. Back safely in Austria, we had a few days in Vienna, where we'd bought an engagement ring decades before, and I did my best to act out as many of the memorable scenes from *The Third Man* as possible, including the celebrated ending when the heroine, Valli (Gerie in this case), walks straight past Joseph Cotton (me) as he waits expectantly in a leaf-denuded avenue.

While still bearing in mind that, in Australia, it was books on the local cinema that were most likely to attract local publishers, and aware that academics are expected to deliver the goods every so often, my La Trobe colleague Geoff Mayer and I proposed to Cambridge University Press (Melbourne chapter) a book to be called *New Australian Cinema: Sources and Parallels in American and British Film*. CUP accepted this proposal and the ensuing book appeared in 1992. One reviewer suggested that it came most vigorously to life when we were writing about American or British film. In my case, charged as I was to make a comparative study of the Australian revival of the 1970s and 80s with the British heyday of the 1940s and 50s, as examples of English-speaking cinemas seeking to establish a national identity and presence in the face of Hollywood's all-conquering dominance of their screen, I embarked on a course of action that would influence the next two decades of my life.

Chapter Nine
Getting to know them

I n 1989, having been commissioned by Cambridge University Press to co-author *New Australian Cinema: Sources and Parallels in American and British Film*, I took myself, with the help of research money, off to London to interview survivors of the heyday of British cinema of the 1940s and 50s, for comparative purposes. I felt I'd lived through the Australian film revival of the 70s, but that I needed first-hand responses from those who'd helped to fashion British cinema's finest hours. This was certainly a more legitimate purpose for such travel than had sometimes been the case.

When writing for *Cinema Papers* during the 1970s and 80s, I'd had some useful experience in interviewing film notables. Peter Weir had fetched up in Melbourne at the time of *Gallipoli*'s release, and my friend Tom Ryan and I went to draw him out about his career to that point. Easy work, actually, with someone as articulate as Weir, but what most impressed my daughter Sophie and her friend was that a young and handsome Mel Gibson was in the room throughout the interview. 'Did you really speak to him?' they asked with wonder in their voices — and a new respect for me. Others caught while promoting their latest films in Australia were two contrasting British actors, both involved with Agatha Christie: the very nice but rather reserved Edward Fox, starring then in *The Mirror Crack'd*, and whose reticence led to the honing of an interviewer's skills; and Sir Peter Ustinov, playing Christie's Belgian bore, Hercule Poirot, in *Evil Under the Sun*. With Ustinov, it was really no more than a matter of pressing Button A and out it all came in fluent, probably oft-repeated sentences. Joan Fontaine was in Melbourne with a view to setting up a stage production of *The Lion in Winter*, a project which never got off the ground. At sixty-three, she was still remarkably beautiful and elegant, and she was an interviewer's dream. Having taken no refuge in either charm or nostalgia, she simply said what she wanted to — for instance, dismissing the great Billy Wilder for whom she appeared in one of his worst films, *The Emperor Waltz* (1947), with 'He was just a guy who'd played the piano in a whorehouse in Vienna, wasn't he?' She later wrote to say she was pleased with the published interview, perhaps partly pleased because we'd contrived not to mention sister and rival Olivia de Havilland once. In 1982 director Lindsay Anderson, who'd had such a critical and commercial success with *If...* back in 1968, was in Melbourne to publicise *Britannia Hospital*, the third in his state-of-the-nation trilogy (*O Lucky Man!*, 1973, was the second). I can't now be quite sure how I came by this interview as it wasn't published in *Cinema Papers* and in fact didn't appear until 1988 in the now-defunct *Filmviews*, by which time I'd got to know Anderson better and could add a lot more of his trenchant views. I'll come back to him.

However, the most influential of these early Melbourne-based interviews, in the light of the work I'd go on to do, was that with English actor Michael Craig who, in 1989, was appearing with Paul Eddington in a production of Terence Rattigan's *The Browning Version* at the Comedy Theatre. By this time I'd begun thinking about my share in the writing of the co-authored book and grabbed the chance to talk to someone who'd had a successful career in British cinema's prolific 1950s. By 1989, he had lived in Australia for nearly two decades and become a household name as the silver-haired surgeon in the ABC's long-running medical-soap series, *GP*. Astute and often cynical about how British cinema had so often played safe, repeating itself with Technicolor comedies set in the Home Counties, when the threat to the leading couple was perhaps a Scandinavian blonde *au pair*, he ended by giving me five hours of considered commentary. What he had to say about

Sir John Davis, Rank's henchman, might, if published, have kept us in litigation for some years. One of the least dangerous of his recollections was of a curious edict of Davis's against the wearing of suede shoes in the Pinewood restaurant. (I met and interviewed Davis two years later in London, by which time he'd become almost benign, as we chomped our way through three courses at the Piccadilly Hotel. 'It doesn't matter. They know me there. I used to own it,' he said when I asked exactly where I should find him). Michael was one of those actors whose grasp of film went considerably beyond his own performances to an understanding of the contextual forces at work in the production of the films he was in. He believed that, though he was busy throughout the 50s, he became type-cast as nice young middle-class professionals, so that he was passed over by the 'new wave' directors, such as Karel Reisz and Lindsay Anderson, whose films were marketing a rougher honesty, and for whom Craig would very much like to have worked.

Very helpfully, when I told him of my plans to go to England to research the book, he put me in touch with such other influential figures in British cinema of the period of my interest as Bryan Forbes, Richard Attenborough, Ian Carmichael and his own very interesting brother, the agent Richard Gregson, who became an important behind-the-scenes figure in the 60s, prior to going to Hollywood, where he married Natalie Wood. To my considerable surprise, all of these people replied and agreed to see me. Philip French, film critic of London's *Observer* who had interviewed me in Australia re my 1986 book, suggested other names — star Virginia McKenna, ace character player Raymond Huntley, director Muriel Box etc — whom I approached with similarly happy results. Thus encouraged, I took to trawling through *Who's Who* for addresses or checked out who was appearing on the stage and fired off requests to the appropriate theatres to, say, Richard Todd and, years later, to Susan Hampshire and Susannah York. Once in London, it was possible to track down yet others via the *Spotlight Casting Directory*, though it must be added that, in an uncertain world, nothing is surer than this: no agent will ever forward a letter to a previous client. Over the next decade I interviewed about 150 persons connected with the British film industry, and this involved an immense amount of letter-writing. I would write asking for an interview; they would reply and I would then write to thank them. Then, nearer the time there would be a further exchange to arrange exact times and places; after the event would be another thank-you (and the courtesies seemed important to me as these people were doing me favours); back in Australia the interviews were typed up and sent to the luminaries for checking, more thanks would ensue, etc, etc. My contribution to the postal revenues of two nations has yet to be fully recognised.

The first interviews were conducted with the shape of the CUP book in mind: that is, the comparison of British cinema of the 40s and 50s with the Australian revival of the 70s, as two English-speaking cinemas in search of a national identity, however consciously or not such an enterprise might have been undertaken. It became clear to me quite early in my 1989 visit that the interviewees were giving me so much — and such interesting — information that it seemed a pity for this to be relegated to footnotes in an academic text, with or without a colon in its title. The interview material deserved a wider audience than this in my view. With this in mind, I approached the British Film Institute (BFI) about the possibility of publishing a separate volume in which these people would be allowed their say in their own voices. The upshot of this was the appearance in 1992 of a rather handsome-looking volume called *Sixty Voices: Celebrities Recall the Golden Age of British Cinema*. I didn't care for the subtitle but was told that it would attract buyers, and I was certainly not opposed to that. As to the main title, it was misleading in the sense that there were sixty-five interviewees, but again I was told that it was better to settle for a 'round figure' in the title.

This book was launched with some style in the handsome rooms of the Royal Society in John Adam Street, London, and a heartening number of the interviewees turned up. There were, among twenty others, Roy Boulting, Ann Todd, Marius Goring, ninety-two-year-old director Harold French, Tony Havelock-Allan, Michael Relph, Dora Bryan, Jean Kent, Harry Fowler, Muriel Pavlow and Sylvia Syms, the latter en route to appearing on stage in Noël Coward's hitherto unstaged *Post-Mortem*. Sylvia wanted 'a family photo with Brian and Gerie' before she left, and as we posed she instructed us that 'shit', not 'cheese', was what you said to ensure maximum effect.

Doing as we were told: Gerie, Sylvia Syms, Brian

We've never forgotten this valuable advice. At one point in this starry evening, I was talking to an old friend with my back to the door. I became aware of a sudden lowering of the noise level, when the friend whispered, 'The Profumos have just come in.' Turning round, I saw Valerie Hobson and husband, former politician John Profumo, around whom a sort of gap had formed. They were without doubt the most glamorous pair I'd ever seen: I don't mean 'glamour' in any conventional Hollywood sense, but more as D.H. Lawrence had in mind when he referred to certain characters as effortlessly exuding a sense of style, confidence and grace. They were two of the most attractive people I'd met, and Valerie, so often patricianly chilly on screen, was a woman of unaffected warmth and friendliness. The gap around them closed, but its fleeting effect was to announce the presence of genuinely superior people.

By this time, I was hooked on the idea of oral testimony as a primary source of film history and just went on doing it after the first book was published. Also, I must admit I just liked meeting these people who had nourished my obsession over the several decades since I'd come to know about them in the pages of *Picture Show*. And sometimes I could scarcely believe that I *was* in the presence of these people only dreamed about as a Wimmera schoolboy. I knew it wasn't a history of hard facts that I was producing as a result of these meetings. It wasn't going to be a history in the way that books quoting documents about, say, studios or legislation relating to film distribution were. It wasn't even going to be a sort of critical history whose main concern was to trace the contours of British film as an art form. Of course I was given a lot of reliable information as well as some shrewd critical assessments, but essentially my interviewees were offering their *perceptions* of how it had been to work in British cinema in those crucial decades — how *they* recalled it to have been. Perceptions can sometimes seem as revealing as statistics. What did seem to be emerging was a sort of mosaic history, with some accounts complementing others or overlapping or even contradicting what others had said.

Triple-Oscar-winning cameraman Freddie Young had started his career in 1917 and I worked my way (other books intervening) up to a present that included the likes of Ken Loach and Anthony Minghella. In between, there was the unalloyed joy of meeting, and in some cases making friends with, the likes of Julie Christie, Roy Boulting, Jean Kent, Valerie Hobson, Lindsay Anderson, Judi Dench, Dirk Bogarde, Richard Attenborough, Sylvia Syms, John

Olive Dodds, felt it might lead to something very important for me. So I agreed to meet Mr Losey and he ran *The Prowler* for me. I saw about twenty-four minutes of it and then told him I'd do the film.

So I joined forces with Joe; Alexis Smith came over from America and she was shattered when she arrived at my house to see Joe sitting there; she had thought the director's name was Vic Hanbury, which was Joe's pseudonym. She was very concerned at making the film with him, given the charges of 'un-American activities' against him, but she stayed – and stayed my friend ever since, a wonderful woman. So we made the film and it was a success; Joe made a lot of money. He was hounded around England by Ginger Rogers and her mother, who were in London at the time, making a film with Stanley Baker. Joe and I didn't work together then for about ten years, although I got him a contract at Rank, which he just about forgave me for, finally!

The Servant is still one of the most engrossing films of the 1960s. What did you find impressive about working with Losey?

It's what I said to you earlier: working with Joe is the way I have worked with all great directors. He would say, 'I don't know what you can do,' and I'd say, 'All right, I'll think of something,' and do it. *The Servant* was wonderful for a stage actor because of the long, long takes – you had a whole magazine of time to do your thing. Sometimes, working with other directors in England, you were very lucky if you could say, 'We got eighty seconds of film for a day's work.' With Joe you got ten minutes, so it was possible to make a film in five weeks. *The Servant* took six weeks to make and Joe was ill for two of them.

There was a lot of very elaborate setting up for it, of course. That film was the only time the dolly-pusher has been given a main credit. There is one scene with Wendy Craig and myself, when I let her in the front door and we go around the drawing room and then into the kitchen, where I fill up the jar with some flowers, then back into the drawing room; I think there were something like forty different camera angles and he never got them wrong. And the lighting was incredible – we took all day but it didn't matter. We would rehearse for about three hours in the morning and the lighting man would say, 'I can't do it,' and Joe would say, 'Yes you can.' Then he would disappear and we wouldn't see each other again until five o'clock in the afternoon, and then we would shoot the whole

thing in an hour. Douglas Slocombe [director of photography], in tears on the last day of shooting, said this was the first time he had been able to put into practice all the things he had learned, and he was never so happy in his life. What's more, he got the Oscar. There was no elaborate set; it was simply the house, an actual house in Chelsea, and Joe uses the house as the metaphor all the way through.

I took over the direction while Joe was in hospital for two weeks. He staggered back early, with a nurse, and picked up. He did not re-shoot anything I had shot, which was what we had hoped. He gave me minute instructions, by telephone, on every set-up. We knew The Money wanted to close us down and grab the insurance. We saved them from doing that. All the companies hated Joe and me because they swore that audiences, seeing our names, left the theatre knowing we were 'art house'. No wonder we finally gave in after five films together!

Did it seem to you that the film was a metaphor for what was happening in British society at the time?

No, it never occurred to me, I just thought it was a great camp joke. I still think it's a very black comedy. It's very disturbing and complex as you say, if you think about it, but it is still a marvellous film which doesn't date. It was a brilliantly written script by Harold Pinter and it was the first script he ever wrote for the movies. When I first read it I didn't know what the hell it was about. I had agreed to go in as co-producer with Joe on it when he first found the book ten years before. It was originally planned that I would play Tony, the nice young man, but then I found the boy, James Fox, here on television. I was too old by that time to play the young man, so I said to Joe we should get Ralph Richardson for the servant. Joe said we couldn't afford it, so that's how I came to play the servant.

The only criticism I would make of the film is that the orgy seems a bit tame by orgy standards today.

Well, when we did that it was the first time we had understood what was happening with LSD parties. Joe and I knew they were taking place, particularly around Chelsea, but the audiences and the critics didn't know. They expected an orgy to involve people screwing each other and they simply didn't understand at the time that it was people going off into space under the influence of an hallucinatory drug – perhaps doing unspeakable things to the boy, but . . . Since then, the critics have reconsidered it in light of their understanding of

Extract from interview with Dirk Bogarde
(An Autobiography of British Cinema, 1997)

Mills, Wendy Hiller, Glenda Jackson, Peter Ustinov, Roy Ward Baker, etc, etc … As Shakespeare in *Twelfth Night* so very nearly said, 'If this be research … give me excess of it.' Furthermore, this was seen as highly respectable research by my university and, indeed, by the

Australian Government: could the latter, I wondered, have misread my grant application in some way when it awarded me a valuable grant to assist this project? But it was not for me to query its munificence, and in 1997 Methuen and the BFI published a sort of 'son of Sixty Voices' called An Autobiography of British Cinema, which contained 135 interviews and a further 55 'profiles' of those who had died or sought less terminal ways to avoid me. The title was my publisher's idea and it seemed a good one, as the point of the book was that it was essentially a series of first-person accounts by people who'd helped make British cinema what it was over seven decades. While film criticism had been my primary interest for such a long time, I realised I was now embarking on another aspect of my writing about film — i.e. as a species of historian/chronicler.

Choosing the people to interview was the obvious starting-point — and finding out if they were willing to see an antipodean obsessive. Actually, I think that being an Australian probably gave me an advantage; it perhaps sounded more exotic to be seeking them out from Melbourne than from, say, Leeds. The bottom line was, of course, whether they would see me, and some persistently evaded me. Jean Simmons, who had so memorably sung 'Let him go, let him tarry' in The Way to the Stars, was the prime example of those I missed out on. I wanted some star names to help sell the book, but it was just as fascinating to me to track down those character players who had always been such a major source of delight in British films (and to whom I'd always given star billing in the University journal I'd co-authored). Or the people behind the camera who contributed so much to what was up there on the screen and sometimes had a more global view of the filmmaking processes than the actors, or to those who were knowledgeable about cinema as an industry. I wanted, too, to meet people who'd made documentaries, art-house filmmakers and B-movie directors.

I've suggested above some of the sources (and addresses) but I was also grateful to those who'd pass me on to others they thought might interest me. Like Julie Christie suggesting I get in touch with director Sally Potter and telling me how to do so. Dinah Sheridan, star of *Genevieve*, asked me if I'd like to meet the director Harold French. I suppressed my astonishment that he was still alive, as he hadn't made a film since *The Man Who Loved Redheads* in 1955, and I heard her say on the phone, 'Harold darling, I have this nice young Australian here who'd like to meet you.' Forget 'nice' and 'Australian', I thought, but 'young'! I was so moved. Or director Lewis Gilbert getting on to Sylvia Syms (whose agent had been quite uncooperative), suggesting that I was quite harmless and she should see me. Valerie Hobson rightly thought it was important for me to speak to her ex-husband Anthony Havelock-Allan, producer of some of the prestige British films of the 1940s, including *Brief Encounter* and *Great Expectations* and gave me his address. In 1990 at a conference in Salisbury, Maryland, I was having lunch with the British documentary filmmaker, Stephen Peet, who asked me what I was planning to do when I went on to England. When I told him, he leant over the table and uttered the magical words, 'I could put you in touch with Nova Pilbeam,' the celebrated teenage star of the 1930s and 40s. She'd starred for Hitchcock among others, but hadn't filmed since 1948 and lived very quietly in North London. Getting to meet this legendary figure, a woman of sharp intelligence, modesty and integrity, was one of the highlights of the whole enterprise for me. A further result of meeting Stephen Peet was that he invited me to a meeting of the ACTT, the Association of Cinema and Television Technicians, which led me to interview Ealing editor-producer Sidney Cole and put me in the way of meeting the eloquent character actress Jean Anderson.

I was particularly keen to interview the actress Kay Walsh (famously Queenie in *This Happy Breed* and Nancy in *Oliver Twist*) but was having no luck in tracking her down. Then Lindsay Anderson, by now a friend and mentor, said, 'If you ring [the producer] Michael Medwin, he is in touch with [film historian and director] Kevin Brownlow, who is currently researching a biography of David Lean and has been talking to Kay Walsh [Lean's second wife].' I followed this trail, picking up interviews with Medwin and Brownlow along the way, and subsequently had four of the most entertaining hours of my life with Walsh. Don't think it was easy arriving at this point. I was staying in a flat in Kensington from which the phone had been disconnected, the previous incumbents having absconded to Tunisia owing British Telecom £875. Early one Monday morning after I'd been there for ten days putting up with this communication problem, two chaps in white boiler-suits came to the door and said they'd come to fix the silent phone. They just flicked the switch and all was well. I could have done it myself if I'd known. Five minutes later the phone rang and a voice said: 'Is that Dr McFarlane? Well this is a person called Kay Walsh here and if your phone is on it is entirely due to me. I got in touch with British Telecom and said to them, "When are you boys going to be out there to reconnect this phone?" and they said, "I think we should probably make it by, say, mid afternoon, about three-ish on Monday." "No good," I said. "I know you chaps; you get out there at three, you say, "Oh it's me tea break," and off you go and you're never seen again. No," I said, "Dr McFarlane's phone has got to be on first thing this morning. This is a very serious heart condition we're talking here."' And so she succeeded where neither I nor the landlady had, which just shows what acting skills can do for you. Further, she said, 'You can come here on Thursday evening.' I said, 'I'm seeing Dame Wendy Hiller at Beaconsfield at 4 o'clock …' 'That's all right,' said Kay. 'Wendy'll be whacked by six o'clock and you can easily get here by seven. I'll give you a sandwich.' And she did. I was rarely more entertained.

As for the interviews themselves, while the earliest ones were geared to the Anglo-Australian comparative study I was engaged in, they became more individually focussed when the BFI announced its intention to publish them separately. I used their careers as a basis, so my preparation was above all to ensure I was absolutely familiar with their work. This involved making exhaustive lists of their credits, with relevant personnel and scraps of information jotted down, and questions prepared. For the popular character actor, Maurice

Denham, I'd prepared a list of 105 film titles, a matter I pointed out with simple pride. 'Ah, but you've missed one,' he said, 'that my scenes were cut from.' It seemed to me that they had the right to expect me to be fully prepared. The actress Ann Todd (whose 1946 film, *The Seventh Veil*, you may recall, was the first my sister and I were allowed to go to at night unattended) told me of an interviewer who had been to see her just a week or so earlier and had settled himself down with a large whisky (as I was about to do), and then said, 'Tell me what you've done.' 'No,' she very properly replied, 'you go away and *find out* what I've done; then come back and ask me about it.' There's surely no point in wasting time asking about what can be easily discovered in advance. My only trick as an interviewer was to let drop early on an esoteric bit of information, not to show off but to indicate that they didn't have to explain everything from scratch. Starting with their careers seemed to work best, encouraging them to branch out where appropriate. This seemed on the whole to produce better results than leading with large questions about the strengths and weaknesses of the British film industry as they saw them. I gave them the final say about what was published because I wanted them to stand by anything that got published. I know it's not then pure oral history, as purists might reasonably object, but it means, 'This is what I think is right.' I remember saying to Kay Walsh, 'You can cut out anything you don't like' and she said reflectively, 'I'll cut out anything nasty I've said about other people … unless it's true.'

I was interested primarily in how they'd gone about pursuing their careers, what sort of training they'd had, how they'd got into films in the first place, whether they preferred the stage to the screen and how they regarded television, what they'd thought about Hollywood and Americans they'd worked with. And so on. Out of such questionings, when my aim was merely to nudge their recollections, I gradually got a sense of the larger contours of British cinema. I wanted these interview books to indicate the *range* of British filmmaking from the obvious prestige points (*Henry V*, *Brief Encounter*, etc) through the wildly popular (Norman Wisdom, the 'Carry On'

movies) to the 'B' films that were part of the programme when I was
growing up (these would be the subject of a later book I co-authored
and which appeared in late 2009). Though the past threw up so
much to admire, it seemed important not just to *linger* there when a
good deal of exciting work was being done in the present day. To this
end, my second interview book, *An Autobiography of British Cinema*
(1997) chronicled encounters with contemporary directors such as
Peter Greenaway, Sally Potter, Ken Loach, Mike Leigh and the late
Anthony Minghella (*The English Patient*), who had the last words
in the book. I wanted too to give some idea of how British cinema
functioned as industry as well as an art, and this led me to seek out
producers, of course, studio heads and agents, who gave a different
perspective. I was interested in getting a wide range of opinions and
perceptions about key films and key personnel, and the result was
some overlap, some corroboration and some contradiction. I decided
to let this stand. This was not, after all, a formal history but a history
composed of disparate, sometimes interlocking, recollections, but,
in their way, history just the same.

When we got to London in 1989, my first visit was to see the
actress Rosamund John and this seemed peculiarly appropriate as
she was the very first British actress I'd ever seen on the screen. She'd
played R.J. Mitchell's (Leslie Howard) wife in *The First of the Few*,
and I'd always remembered her gently nursing him as he sat dying in
his garden, exhausted, as you would be, after inventing the Spitfire.
She was in fact always being described as a 'gentle-mannered' actress,
whereas she was much more tough-minded than that would suggest.
A vigorous Labourite, as a result, she claimed, of her school study of
the Industrial Revolution, she'd married the Labour politician John
Silkin who'd come to canvass her — in mistake, she said, for Glynis
Johns (who eluded me by being in Los Angeles when I couldn't get
there). Mostly these interviews took place in the flats and houses
where they lived, but there were some notable exceptions, such as the
cafeteria of the National Theatre for Judi Dench, who couldn't utter
the title of *Macbeth* because of the superstition banning its use on

theatrical premises. The interview with Honor Blackman began over breakfast in Fortnum and Mason's until she became nervous that her car might be clamped, so we finished our talk sitting in the car in St James's Square. And there was the House of Commons, where I interviewed Glenda Jackson, after first being frisked for bombs. I liked being thought potentially dangerous. There were other meetings in cafés (Gordon Jackson, kind and charming to autograph hunters as we sat at tea in Louis', Hampstead), the plushy interiors of London clubs (director Ralph Thomas, actors Marius Goring, Moira Shearer, John Mills and several others). Some who persisted in being in the wrong continent had to be 'done' by phone, which produced some very astute self-criticism from director Val Guest in Palm Springs and less of this from Vanessa Redgrave in Houston.

Though my university was generous about allowing me time for these projects (and also helped with funding them), I never had quite as much time as I'd have liked. This meant that I had to turn down the invitations of director Guy Hamilton to visit him in Mallorca, and of famous 1950s comic Norman Wisdom, then living on the Isle of Man. Both agreed to telephone interviews, and at the time I was just technically proficient enough to manage these. But from 1989 to 1996 I hurtled all over London (from Sid Cole in Ealing in the west, [Lord] Bernard Miles in the east, James Fox in the south, and screenwriter Diana Morgan at Denville Hall, the theatricals' retirement home, in the north), to Coventry to interview actor Richard Todd in his dressing-room at the theatre, to Pinewood Studios to meet producers Betty Box and husband Peter Rogers, to Brighton for wonderful character actress Dora Bryan, to Hove for Carmen Dillon, doyenne of production designers, to Suffolk for actress Jean Kent, cinematographer Walter Lassally and sound recordist Peter Handford, to Wiltshire for cinematographer Ossie Morris, and to Amersham to see Dulcie Gray and Michael Denison. This last took place in Dulcie Gray's bedroom, where she'd retired to her four-poster of pain but revived wonderfully under the stimulus of talking about her fifty-year career. I'd left London for Amersham just before she'd rung to cancel the interview; I missed Michael Denison who'd gone to the station to meet me, and walked to the elegant John Adam house they lived in; but after this unpromising start they proved very alert interviewees. As well, there were meetings in Melbourne (the popular duo of Googie Withers and John McCallum; the astringent, articulate director Mike Leigh, here to promote *Secrets & Lies*; the genuinely sweet Hayley Mills, appearing on stage in *Fallen Angels*), in Sydney (director Jack Lee and actor Vincent Ball, who had both had careers in England before settling in Australia, where they'd both been involved in filming *A Town Like Alice* and *Robbery Under Arms*), in Malibu, California, where director Ken Annakin's sitting-room seemed to command a view of the entire Pacific Ocean, and Deauville, France, where I finally ran director Ronald Neame to earth, after a demanding two-day journey in a hire car from Salzburg.

It's not possible to list here all the people who made themselves available. They were almost uniformly courteous, friendly, and often hospitable beyond the call of — well, not exactly duty, but of co-operation. They offered lunch, tea, drinks: looking back, I can hardly believe I had tea (including a genuine home-made Victoria sponge) with Wendy Hiller, or lunch with those great cameramen, Freddie Young and Ossie Morris, or drinks with Dirk Bogarde ('I bought the couch you're sitting on from Coral Browne for fifty quid', he told me), or that I took John Mills to lunch. As to the latter, he proved to be a very slow eater (and in my own family I am cruelly berated for my own slowness), partly because he kept telling me such interesting things over his salmon steak while I didn't have my cassette recorder on, and I could see my actual interview time diminishing as he had to get a 3 pm train back to Denham. Pursuit of Rank's highly successful producer Betty Box led my wife and me to Pinewood Studios, but not by anything as commonplace as public transport. Betty said when I was confirming the meeting, 'Oh, don't think of coming by train. People have been known to come to Uxbridge Station and never been seen again. I'll send a car for you.' A chauffeur arrived at 9 am at our Kensington flat and skilfully negotiated the western suburbs, getting us to Pinewood in time for a tour of the studios before lunch. *Batman* had recently been filmed there and the Gotham City street sets were still standing, and we saw the tank in which the 'Titanic' had been sunk in Roy Ward Baker's 1958 film, *A Night to Remember.* Betty's husband, producer Peter Rogers, whom I interviewed the next year, was also at lunch in the luxurious flat attached to the studios, and after the interview itself the car returned us to Kensington. I have to say that this spoilt me for train and bus travel.

I was especially interested in connections between stage and screen as they perceived it. The London stage has long been one of the glories of theatrical history, but I wondered if its proximity to the film studios, unlike in the US where the centres of stage and screen are on opposite sides of the continent, had in some ways inhibited British cinema. Had it perhaps produced a kind of acting that might look too 'big' on the screen? Had the stage's essentially middle-class orientation (in both subject matter and audience appeal) encouraged a stage- and class-bound cinema? Did British actors still regard the stage as their first allegiance, with the cinema as a way of replenishing their coffers? As to the last question, Sir John Gielgud — Lindsay Anderson had paved the way for this interview — was frank in agreeing that this had been his early response. Dora Bryan — and think with how many spiteful hussies and trollops she had enlivened films — still loved the stage best and

After a few more services comedies, such as *Desert Mice*, you had in *A Taste of Honey* what is perhaps the best role of your film career. How did you come by this?

About those services comedies, Basil Dearden directed *Desert Mice* (and *The Blue Lamp*); I think he felt actors got in the way of his films! He was nice to me because I didn't give him any trouble, but generally I don't think he liked actors very much. *A Taste of Honey* was certainly my best film role – *and* I had a script! Helen was really *in* the film, not just a cameo. I've no idea how I came by the role but thank goodness Tony Richardson chose me. Although perhaps I shouldn't say 'thank goodness' because I didn't do many films after that. I enjoyed doing that part very much but I didn't realise the film would be such a success. It was filmed at Salford in Manchester and also in a big attic over two garages in London. The seafront stuff was all shot at Salford Docks. I saw the film again last year and loved it. And it's interesting to see a film in black-and-white now, after everything being in colour for so long; it adds something to it, gives it something of a documentary look. Tony Richardson gave a lot of direction to Rita Tushingham but it was her first film. With me, I think he cast me to be as he sees me. It's funny that, having won a BAFTA award for the film, no one asked me to do any films for such a long time.

You did a couple of thrillers – *Hands of the Ripper* for Hammer was one.

Yes, that was a nice part. I played a medium and I ended up being stabbed through the stomach, then I was hung on the door for a little while.

Extract from interview with Dora Bryan

regarded film as 'the icing on the cake' as she'd trot out to the studios to do her couple of days' work. She claimed she would often have no idea of what the rest of the film was about, having been sent only her own bit of the script or sometimes learnt her part while she was being made-up, and it would be quite a surprise to her if she saw the completed film.

Others, like Michael Hordern, conceding, like so many other actors, that 'I never turned anything down,' drew attention to the exhaustion they felt when they were working in the studios by day and racing back to the West End stages by night. And Margaretta Scott, similarly conceding, said she couldn't remember some of her films. As she said, even if the play you were in failed, you would have rehearsed it for a month and its run would rarely be less than a fortnight, so you were unlikely to have erased all trace of it from your memory, whereas with a film you might just have been needed for two or three days and might not ever have seen the finished product. Wendy Hiller, like several others, disliked the way films were shot out of sequence and the fact that there was too much sitting around, but, as she grew older, she liked the finiteness of filmmaking. With a play, you couldn't predict its run, but with a film you knew how long you were going to be required — and, she added, they so disliked having to pay you for an extra day. 'As I grow older, I like my certain-ties,' she summed up. Kathleen Byron's preference for film was that she liked having everything — make-up, costumes, etc — done for her. She told me this when she was bored with being murdered at the end of Act One of *The Mousetrap* and having to wait around for the curtain call. Even trying to learn Spanish as she was at the time hardly assuaged the tedium, she claimed.

On the whole, the interviews were free from the sort of bitchy comment some reviewers seemed to be hoping for. Over tea in his Pimlico flat, the inimitable character actor Raymond Huntley pointed to my cassette recorder and said, 'Turn off that machine and I'll tell you something really interesting.' And did, but again my distaste for litigation forbids me to quote it. The odd side-swipe would seep through the generally well-mannered demeanour. Actor Dermot Walsh blamed director Charles Crichton for putting paid to his career as a star of 'A' films by deliberately sabotaging a screen test; Crichton, in his turn, dismissed the widely admired Boulting brothers very scathingly, largely because they'd had him removed from directing the film of *Lucky Jim*; producer Daniel Angel characterised Bette Davis as 'a cow', though actors Kay Walsh and Harry Fowler wouldn't have agreed. Kay was, however, sharp about Joan Fontaine, with whom she appeared in *The Witches*, on which she claimed Fontaine had a trailer 'big enough for several third-world families.' Among other Hollywood imports, Gregory Peck and Tyrone Power were universally regarded as a pleasure to work with, minor Warners star of the 1940s, Dane Clark, as an arrogant pain in the neck, and the late Jean Anderson thought Jennifer Jones (on *The Barretts of Wimpole Street*) 'too silly for words ... always afraid she might catch something.' As for those who'd disliked working with the inspired maverick, Michael Powell, their populous ranks included Kathleen Byron, Moira Shearer, Wendy Hiller and Googie Withers, who also recorded her adverse opinion of Alfred Hitchcock's working methods. Googie had no compunction about making her views known to them when she worked on their films in the 1930s: 'I was as assured then [barely twenty] as I am today,' she said and husband John McCallum, passing at this moment, added, 'And that's very assured.' And there was enjoyable sharpness at work in Phyllis Calvert's recollection of co-starring with a very young Richard Burton: 'One day he told me he had saved some money and had just taken out a mortgage on a house. It had three floors; he had the middle flat and he intended to let the upper and lower flats. He said, "I'll never have to work again!" That's sweet isn't it?' They were of course giving me insights into more serious aspects of filmmaking in Britain — its precarious financing, its attempts to emulate the Hollywood star and studio systems, its gradual toe-in-the-water approach to television, its literary and theatrical affiliations and its dealings with the British class system. But this is a (sort of) memoir, not a critical history, so those insights mainly belong — and can be found — elsewhere.

I said earlier that some of those interviewed became friends and this was one of the great bonuses of the 'research'. Take three examples. The BFI launched *Sixty Voices* in late 1992 and also organised three screenings, to be chosen by me, at the Museum of London theatrette, to which I was to invite a key collaborator in each case. The films I chose were: the post-war melodrama *Good Time Girl*, to be introduced by good-time girl herself, Jean Kent; the tale of political idealism gone sour, *Fame Is the Spur*, with director Roy Boulting in attendance; and Powell and Pressburger's masterpiece, *Black Narcissus*, in the presence of Kathleen Byron who'd played Sister Ruth, driven mad by repression and lust in her Technicolor convent high up in the Himalayas (actually Sussex). These three — Jean, Roy and Kathleen — became friends whom we saw on subsequent trips to England. Jean several times did publicity for books of mine, allowing herself to be interviewed again in bookshops for instance, and several times giving us excellent lunches at her Westhorpe home. She also in 2003, and to a rousing welcome, launched my *Encyclopedia of British Film* in London. Roy would take us to meals in restaurants where he was known, refusing lunch at the club to which my university had reciprocal rights. ('Oh, Mac,' he would say dismissively, 'it will be boarding-school food.') As we would eat our way through three delicious courses, he would smoke a great deal, get on with the wine, and toy with an omelette. He was very ill the last time I saw him, in 2000, and living in a council flat out of Oxford, but insisted on taking me to a country pub where, as usual, I had the very good meal he wanted me to have while he mainly watched. As for Kathleen, she was an exceptionally intelligent woman, married to novelist Alaric Jacob, and she asked us to dinner at her east London home where she had prepared blintzes, among other delicacies. 'Blintzes' always conjured up for me the Grand Duchess in *You Can't Take It with You*, which I'd produced at Trinity Grammar School: her one great line was, 'The tsar he always say to me, Olga, do not be stingy with the blintzes.' Sitting next to Kathleen while up on the screen in *Black Narcissus* she was going spectacularly mad was one of life's more memorable, if disconcerting, experiences. Roy, on the other hand, having introduced *Fame Is the Spur* for the audience, turned to me and said, 'Mac, you don't imagine I'm going to sit through it, do you?' and we repaired to a local pub, arriving back just in time for the unsuspecting audience to ply him with questions.

Others whom I/we (Gerie wasn't always as ready to drop everything and fly to England as I was) grew fond of and would see when in London included the director Roy Ward Baker, who lived in Kensington with his partner Lady (Philippa) Astor, a woman of impressive intelligence and an accomplished cook, and Dinah Sheridan who helped with publicity for *An Autobiography of British Cinema* and whose daughter Jenny Hanley, by her marriage to Jimmy Hanley, would interview me years later. As I entered the Saga radio station studio to talk about the *Encyclopedia* in 2003, a nice-looking blonde woman approached me and gave me a kiss, then said, 'My mother told me to do that.' Dinah was then living in California with her now late husband, Aubrey. Anthony Havelock-Allan and his wife Sara were notably hospitable in their Warwick Square apartment; Dirk Bogarde, a stimulating if not wholly reliable interviewee, offered drinks and entertaining chat on several successive visits, and proved to be an indefatigable correspondent, whose often misspelt missives have recently been collected by his brilliant biographer, John Coldstream. And Margaretta Scott, of imperious demeanour in films but warmth and kindness in real life, the witty and ironic Kay Walsh, and the modest Robert S. Baker, B-movie maker and then TV producer, were others whose on-going friendship it was a pleasure to renew from time to time. In Australia, Googie Withers and John McCallum became friends and an on-going source of entertainment and information for twenty years now. A sad duty and privilege was, at John's request, to write a newspaper obituary for him when he became seriously ill in late 2009 and died in the following February.

One who deserves a paragraph or two to himself is the afore-mentioned Lindsay Anderson. 'Trenchant' was absolutely the word I'd apply to Lindsay: 'difficult' and 'impossible' were others that I've heard people use. Perhaps, though, as a result of my being impervi-ous to insult or of his being amused by my devotion to ancient British cinema, we hit it off and I always saw him when we were in England. After having first interviewed him when he was in Australia in 1982 vainly trying to promote *Britannia Hospital*, I had further dealings with him in England in 1984 when I was trying to put together an anthology of the critical writings in *Sequence*, the journal he and others like Gavin Lambert and Karel Reisz had edited in the late 1940s and 50s. This finally failed to materialise because of Lindsay's ingrained (and, no doubt, unwarranted) distrust of the British Film Institute (BFI) which had been interested in such a publication. However, we got on well and I enjoyed his sometimes cantanker-ous company. I remember a couple of occasions when I'd gone out to have lunch at his Finchley Road flat. On one of these, I'd been enthusing about some 1940s British film melodrama, possibly one directed by Lance Comfort or Lawrence Huntington, when I could see his eyes narrow in disapproval. 'Have you no discrimination of any kind?' he asked me. On another day, knowing I'd been watching British films in the archive of the BFI, he asked me what I'd been seeing that morning. I named Bernard Miles's mildly iconoclastic *Chance of a Lifetime*. 'How did you find it?' he asked. 'Oh, it was not uninteresting,' I foolishly ventured. He turned to the other guests at the lunch table (including *If...* screenwriter David Sherwin) and said, 'Not uninteresting! Brian's an academic you know.' No com-pliment was intended. But if you were going to take offence at such comments, then your best plan was simply to stay away. As far as I was concerned, the compensations were considerable: I felt I'd rarely been in the presence of so persistently attentive and discriminating a mind.

When Lindsay first came to dinner with us at the Kensington flat we'd been lent, Gerie, who hadn't met him before, was appalled to hear this curmudgeonly voice coming up the stairs, berating me with, 'You told me it was the *first* entrance away from the Earl's Court Road. It's not; it's the second.' She was wondering what the ensuing evening could possibly be like, but in the event she was charmed by him — and he was charming *to her*, reserving his barbs and narrowed eyes for me. I forget which actress I'd just spoken of in the kindliest, almost reverential terms, when he turned to Gerie and said, 'He *is* soppy, isn't he?' In spite of his socialist views, he had been wary enough to invest in an Australian firm called Coles-Myer.

'Have you ever heard of them?' he asked, unaware that it was possibly the largest retail firm in Australia, and offered Gerie his discount card with the company. Then he thought he should write an authorisation on the back of it, to the effect that he, Lindsay Anderson, authorised Geraldine McFarlane etc. *Then*, he corrected himself to change it to read: 'I Lindsay Anderson *hereby* authorise ...' 'I think 'hereby' makes it sound more official,' he explained. In the event, Gerie once got ten per cent off on a tube of toothpaste as a result of exercising her authority, but he died soon after and so she kept the card merely as a memento. The last time I saw Lindsay was in London just a couple of weeks before his sudden death in France in 1994. To the end he was being critical of the class system in Britain and how it had, in his view, limited the

scope and appeal of British films. That is, he was utterly himself till the end, which came too soon. On subsequent visits to London, I've greatly missed seeing him and having him correct my callow enthusiasms. He had been very kind to me, putting me in the way of interviews, suggesting how I could get in touch with, say, Kevin Brownlow, Alan Bates, James Fox or Harry Fowler, and in the case of character actor Bill Owen even conducting the interview for me, with my questions, because Bill was away filming in Yorkshire while I was actually in England. He was no doubt a combative man, but if many found him too daunting there were certainly many who valued and had reason to be grateful for his friendship, and I was one of these.

In a sense he was a bridge between the survivors of 1940s and 50s British cinema, the period of my earliest research and interviews, and the major changes that were wrought in the often anodyne films of the 50s with the breaking of the 'New Wave' on British shores at the end of the decade. I still went on seeking out people from earlier decades when the chance arose. I mean, I wasn't going to turn down the chance of talking to Linden Travers, gorgeously beautiful in, say, Hitchcock's *The Lady Vanishes,* and especially adept at discreet mistresses. Or director Vernon Sewell, who made his name on … *one of our aircraft is missing* and who happened on his ninety-first birthday to be passing through London from his Durban home on his way to sail his steam yacht in the south of France. As you would. He said he'd never been interviewed before, and he had a memory of bell-like clarity. Increasingly though, with the next book (*An Autobiography of British Cinema*) in mind, I was sending letters to and getting positive replies from the likes of Rita Tushingham, Jack Clayton, Karel Reisz, Alan Bates, James and Edward Fox, Glenda Jackson, Ken Loach — and Julie Christie: names that were associated with a new kind of British film.

If there is one truly iconic image that seemed to me to sum up this latter it was that previously noted sight of Julie Christie swinging her way down a drab northern street in *Billy Liar* and disrupting the expectations of the eponym played by Tom Courtenay (who, like Albert Finney, had turned me down, preferring to get on with the present than to recall the past). At our London flat one Saturday morning, the phone rang and a voice said, 'Is that Dr McFarlane? This is Julie Christie speaking.' Now, I can't imagine many more phone calls I'd rather receive. She was offering to meet me on the following Saturday, by which time I'd have been back in Australia for several days. Bravely overcoming this disappointment, I settled for an hour's phone interview, with which she professed herself so delighted when I sent her the typescript that I ventured to ask her to do a foreword for the book. She tentatively agreed and when I was in London the following year, 1995, I went to see her backstage at the theatre where she was starring in a revival of Pinter's *Old Times*. I reported this meeting to my son, then living in London, telling how she'd held my hand while she spoke. His immature comment was, 'So? She's fifty,' reminding me of what Shaw had said about youth's being wasted on the wrong people. 'Would I like to come and talk further about the book one day next week while she was being made up?' she'd suggested. Well, of course I would and did, and, along with being so obviously one of the great beauties of British (or any) cinema, she also proved to be intelligent and smashingly nice. It seemed as wholly apt to have her name on the cover of this book as it had been to have that of the great Googie Withers on the preceding one.

How did they live, these famous names? In short, agreeably but not in conformity with the Hollywood idea of poolside grandiosity and immense security. The rewards of working in the British film industry, augmented by stage and television, were clearly adequate but within more modest limits. And almost without exception their way of dealing with an interviewer accorded with their surrounds. They seemed remarkably free of oppressive ego, though when I suggested this to agent Richard Gregson, he said, 'Oh, they're on their best behaviour. They can do ego when they need.' Maybe so, but I was

For many people, including me, when you swung down that drab northern street in *Billy Liar*, you seemed to announce a new spirit in British films. How did you feel about the part of Liz?

I can't remember much about the actual part because other factors were much more dominant. One was that at last I was in a New Wave film, an English equivalent to the French stuff, so that I was realising my ambition to be in class (in this case *working*-class!) films, something that aspired to be a reaction against the status quo, which is what I wanted to do most of all because I thought myself a rebel. The other thing I remember was absolute terror, because I hadn't a clue what I was supposed to be doing from beginning to end, although John Schlesinger was very good to me.

Did you share Liz's approach to life?

I can't say I did. Despite the fact I thought of myself as a rebel, I was very shy, and Liz wasn't shy. She was also of a very different class from me, so that when she got lifts from lorry drivers she had the confidence of equality, whereas I would have been absolutely paralysed by my awful middle-classness and unable to say anything at all. In a way it was her class that gave her her strength and I didn't have that class.

Do you think it's a major disappointment that Billy hasn't the nerve to go off with her?

No, not really. When you read a script you understand the aspirations of the film and what you are contributing to, the shape of it, and I was contributing to something the shape of which had to end the way it did. The outcome was very much the point of the film, I think. For all his fantasising, Billy is trapped; he is as conservative as anyone else. I wouldn't agree with John, however, that the ending was triumphant; I think it is a successful ending because it is a truthful one.

You did three major films in the '60s for John Schlesinger, plus the television version of *Separate Tables* in the '80s. What did you like about working with him?

It wasn't so much that we had a good working relationship as that John was so terribly kind and a very dear person. I have a great fondness for him and we understand each other. After *Darling* I think we both understood a lot about each other's weaknesses and faults and that bound us together. It wasn't until I did *Separate Tables* that I was able to relax and really appreciate John as a director. Beforehand I was terrified of the whole acting business, but in *Separate Tables* his skills as a director of actors really struck me – and they worked, because I think I gave a good performance. Some people might say that, considering my unresponsive attitude, his skill with actors was manifest from my first film with him!

What kind of direction did he give?

He gives a lot of direction – he is an actor's director – as opposed to Joe Losey, who doesn't give much direction. Of course John was an actor himself; he knows what he wants and he is jolly well going to get it. He is watching you all the time and, if it's going well, he lets you get on with it. If it's not going well, he is with you and altering it for you.

Darling won a number of Oscars, including yours for Best Actress. It seems to me a key film of the '60s. How do you feel about it today?

I think it is a film of its time. I'd call it very good source material for the '60s. I think it needs a bit more time before I could judge it on a 'forever' basis, but that sharp, slick dialogue grates a bit now. It's a bit too slick, not naturalistic, so I think one would have to wait a bit longer to see it as a product on its own and whether it holds up as a period piece.

I can't think of another film in which the protagonist is such a silly, selfish, superficial character as Diana Scott. Was it a difficult role to play, to keep her interesting?

It wasn't difficult for me, I think it was probably the easiest part I've done! I *was* pretty silly, selfish and superficial then, if I'm not now! I understood a lot of what that silly girl was going through. I did despise that vacuous, empty-headed part of her,

Extract from interview with Julie Christie
(An Autobiography of British Cinema, 1997)

never made to feel that I was being a nuisance or impertinent: the most any said was that they might have to limit the time they could spare. Actors particularly were often enormously entertaining, their facility in mimicry allowing them to evoke people they'd worked with. In this respect though, I think one of the funniest of all was director Ronald Neame's recollection of Edith Evans's carrying all before her when it looked as if she mightn't be going to get the lead in his version of *The Chalk Garden*. A runner-up was the very likable character actor Harry Fowler's acting out of the entire story of *Fire Maidens of Outer Space*, in which he appeared and which he cheerfully described as 'the worst film ever made'. They almost invariably took the trouble to think about the sorts of answers they were giving, and the extra trouble of correcting things they thought they'd got wrong when I sent them the typescripts. I still have director Peter Greenaway's amended script with almost two hundred small corrections. Even those who said, 'It was all too long ago, I won't remember anything, you know,' would respond to this or that bit of information I'd recalled or found when preparing for the interviews.

I've done a lot of research since, but none, whatever its considerable rewards, has ever been as wholly enjoyable as coming face to face with so many people who were, to me at least, legendary names, names I'd revered since distant boyhood. Only one was diminished in my eyes as a result of making such contact (by international phone in the middle of my night as it happened) and on this subject my lips are sealed. This person asked condescendingly, in the spirit of one making a recondite suggestion, if I knew a journal called *Sight and Sound* as this would help me to brush up my ideas. I could only reply, 'Yes, I've been subscribing to it for forty years.' More common was the experience I had of talking to someone like Richard Attenborough who made me feel he'd been waiting for years for this chance to chat. In this case, in fact, it was I who called the interview to a halt as it had gone on for three times as long as his secretary had said he'd be available.

An Autobiography of British Cinema was finally launched in the Museum of the Moving Image in London's National Film Theatre, and again an encouraging number of the interviewees turned up to make a memorable occasion of it. My daughter-in-law videoed chunks of the evening, so that one can see, for example, director Ken Annakin and actress Linden Travers greeting each other rapturously for the first time since Ken had directed her in one of the stories in Somerset Maugham's *Quartet*, nearly fifty years earlier. Roy Boulting was there, politely incredulous when told he couldn't smoke; Sylvia Syms, who offered to do publicity, was in a shimmering gold outfit; Maurice Denham, Jean Kent, Dinah Sheridan, heroically present when she was heading for the US next morning, Rona Anderson (queen of British second features), then terminally-ill Marius Goring, directors Roy Ward Baker and Peter Graham Scott and cinematographer Ossie Morris and Oscar-winning costume designer Julie Harris (who had spoken of actresses who wouldn't know *haute couture* from *haute cuisine*) were among the others who turned up and threw themselves into the night's entertainment. So did Rita Tushingham who next day came with me and the Methuen publicist to Manchester to flog the book at a Waterstone's Bookshop lunch at which we shared the platform with Nigel Nicholson, Max Bygraves and politician Roy Hattersley, who were all peddling memoirs of various kinds. On the publicity trail Sylvia Syms and I were being interviewed live on television, when my sycophantic contribution to the occasion was to refer to well-known director 'X' who'd several times used Sylvia in character roles. I'd said to him, 'I think Sylvia Syms is on the verge of being a great character actress.' 'She's *not*, she *is* a great character actress,' he countered. 'That's interesting,' Sylvia said, 'because I can't stand X.' 'My dear, you speak for the nation,' said chat-show hostess Jane. With that sure instinct for self-preservation that comes to our rescue sometimes, I thought: 'These two could be sued but I haven't said a word out of place.'

It was at a celebratory lunch with Methuen people some days after this launch that the question of the need for an encyclopedia of British film came up. Actually, I think it may have been I who raised it. It *was*. But there was some enthusiasm for this project, the lack of such a volume's basic information having caused me a lot more work in preparing interviews. Anyway, this idea would later lead me to an enterprise that would keep me off the streets for five years.

Chapter Ten
Putting it down and getting it all together

The last ten years of my teaching career were almost wholly a matter of pleasure. Shorn of most of the administrative work which bored me and for which I had only the most limited skills, I felt I was being paid to do the things I enjoyed: teaching, researching and writing. Certainly there were tedious batches of essays and exams regularly spaced through the semester, but if this was the worst that might be said of a job then I think I was lucky. To work among agreeable people, doing pretty much what I liked best, seems to me the height of privilege, and I kept doing it until 31 December 1999, the date supposed by the ignorant populace to be the end of the millennium. After this, realising I had no gifts for retirement, I simply wrote full-time and still do.

During the last couple of decades as an academic, I was teaching in both literature and film and, in pursuit of a major research interest, film-and-literature in relation to the phenomenon of adaptation. After teaching a subject in the latter area a few times, I decided to research it further for my PhD thesis, which led to the book I've referred to previously, *Novel to Film*. I was bored with the common responses that might have been summed up as 'It wasn't like that in the book', as though a filmmaker were obliged, in adapting a novel, to offer the same experience as the reader had had in reading the book — as if this were even possible, let alone desirable. For those who want the same experience, I could only recommend re-reading the novel, though even then … I kept thinking of Orson Welles's opinion that, if a filmmaker had nothing new to say about a novel (or other work of literature) he'd best leave it alone.

Quite a bit of my writing in the 1990s was on this subject, but I also became involved in co-editing the *Oxford Companion to Australian Film*. This proved to be a massive undertaking, including a fraught period involving a change of co-editor, but settled enjoyably when the editing trio was completed by La Trobe University colleagues and friends, Geoff Mayer and Ina Bertrand. Ina's expert grasp of early Australian cinema plugged gaps in Geoff's and my first-hand knowledge, and the over-all result was handsome and readable. It attracted some heartening reviews, including a page in *Time* magazine, along with its share of local sniping, especially from people who hadn't been asked to contribute to it, and especially from one whose agent had demanded ten times what Oxford was able to pay. The pleasures of writing entries in a book such as this include the sheer finiteness of the activity: you know you can only have a certain number of words; the research for each entry is intense and brief, then you move on to the next; and over-all you hope some sense of the field as a whole, in this case Australian cinema, will emerge.

The point about 'finiteness' also applies to reviewing, and in the last thirty years I've done a great deal of this. Not only has the review to be done by a certain, imminent date and within a word-limit, but it also characteristically attracts a fee. As an academic, I was prepared to pay my dues in the form of articles in scholarly 'refereed' journals, and even to enjoy researching and writing some of them, then adding them carefully to my CV and to the English Department's annual list of publications, which in turn would attract crucial extra funds. Such articles have included pieces on David Lean's *Great Expectations*, on the great MGM romantic melodrama, *Random Harvest*, on Peter Bogdanovich's undervalued film version of Henry James's *Daisy Miller*, on recent film versions of Ian McEwan's *Atonement* and Evelyn Waugh's *Brideshead Revisited*, all drawing on my interest in the processes and reception of novel-film adaptation, as well as literary articles on such Australian novelists as Henry Handel Richardson, Patrick White and Martin Boyd and the inimitable English novelist Ivy Compton-Burnett. From the late 1970s, I was writing more and more about film, with the lively, now-defunct journal *Cinema Papers* providing a very congenial forum. Much of the reviewing here was related to Australian films, enjoying a new buoyancy in the revival of the 70s. I was often asked to review films with a literary lineage (e.g., *The Getting of Wisdom, My Brilliant Career, The Mango Tree, Monkey Grip*) and eventually this led to the book *Words and Images*, published jointly by Heinemann and Cinema Papers and launched in conjunction with the John Grierson Memorial Lecture in 1983. I chose to talk about novel-film connections on this occasion and can't think that Grierson, the austere old founder of the documentary movement, would have been in the least impressed. Looking back, I now wonder if this preponderance of films derived from prestigious novels was seen as a short-cut to aesthetic respectability in the new Australian cinema, but that didn't trouble me at the time.

But, as I said, I really do find reviewing one of the most compelling activities. At least, I can say I virtually never turn any such offers down, whether of books or films. As the *Australian Book Review* reported when I was its 'Critic of the Month' in 2006, after writing of previous careers as teacher and academic: 'Now, third, he has become a writer, and writing incessantly is what he does — when, that is, he is not reading the books and watching the films he needs to read or watch in order to write about them. A chronic incapacity to say No to anything attractive means that he usually has more to do than is good for, say, home-maintenance chores'. This piece went on to say why I found reviewing so attractive: 'When he knows he should be researching and arguing his way through a chapter in a book, the publication date of which looms but about which he feels strangely unwilling to tap out the opening lines, it is relief to turn to an enjoyable task which [he] knows must be done within a few days and within a tightly specified length'. Which is just another way of talking about its finiteness.

COMMENTARY

Resisting Tarantino

A seminal year in Australian cinema

by Brian McFarlane

In 2004, *Somersault*, a drama of youthful coming to terms with life's challenges, scooped the pool at the Australian Film Institute's annual awards. It was a melancholy comment on the state of the local industry that no other films could compete with this affecting but scarcely remarkable work. How different the situation will be in 2009.

Whether one film walks off with all the major awards or not, there has not been such a line-up of notable Australian films in a single year since the 1970s revival began with *Wake in Fright*, now screening to considerable acclaim in a new print. I haven't seen every Australian film this year, but those I have suggest it is an *annus mirabilis*. Run your eye over this list: *Mary & Max, Samson & Delilah, Disgrace, Blessed, My Year Without Sex, Bastardy, The Cedar Boys, Last Ride, Beautiful Kate* and *Balibo*. Any one of these deserves serious notice; taken as a job lot, they are extraordinary.

What, if anything, have they in common, apart from their critical success? It would be easy to say that individuality is their distinguishing characteristic, but this doesn't get us far. They seem, though, to have been made, whatever gross commercial considerations impelled their backers, without surrendering creative integrity to the satisfying of conventional expectations or box-office potential. There is a note of guarded optimism at the end of, say, *Disgrace* or *Samson & Delilah*, but that doesn't erase all trace of what has disturbed us in the preceding hour or so. I don't mean that these are merely 'quirky' films (I regard 'quirky' as only slightly less dubious than the dreaded 'feisty'): they are all serious, though not solemn, in their pursuit of a sustaining, personal idea or – indeed – vision.

They are a long way from the 'franchise' school of cinema, which probably requires resources beyond the reach of any of the film-makers concerned. Just think what good might be achieved by the distribution of the budgets needed for the *Harry Potter* or *Spiderman* series to the needy of the world. But this is to digress. The films listed above are essentially art-house rather than multiplex in their orientation and exhibition, though that distinction is no longer clear-cut. At Melbourne's Cinema Nova, for example, *Samson & Delilah* rubs shoulders with Johnny Depp and Harry Potter.

It is unequivocally true that all these films are intended for adults. One doesn't have to submit to a comic-strip surface on the off chance of a serious subtext or the 'darker' implications of digitally conceived high jinks precariously strung together as plot. Instead, these films offer narratives thematically welded by potent issues of race and ethnicity in *Disgrace, Bastardy, Samson & Delilah* and *Cedar Boys*, of parent-child relations in *Last Ride, Beautiful Kate* and *Blessed* (films that question what 'home' might mean), of political tyranny and cover-up in *Balibo*, and of loneliness and how it might be assuaged in *Mary & Max*. These aren't just issues-driven films, but they have more in mind than killing time painlessly.

Four of the listed films are feature débuts. Warwick Thornton's *Samson & Delilah* is a triumph of compassionate and rigorous film-making. In contrast with the baroque inanities of Baz Luhrmann's *Australia*, Thornton, the director, exercises an austere hand over Thornton the cinematographer. We are perhaps a half hour into the film before the camera pulls back to take in the whole Aboriginal community in which the action has been taking place. It is the people – Samson (Rowan McNamara), waking, sniffing petrol; Delilah (Marissa Gibson), making a fire, waking an old woman and these two getting on with their painting – that matter; the location gradually emerges through their interaction with it. This is executed with minimum dialogue and in calm, unfussy visual terms. If there are vestigial elements of romantic comedy in the way the couple is being set up, we can't take comfort from such a genre echo. There is no sentimentality in Thornton's unsparing and non-exploitatative account of tough lives – there are brief moments of ugly violence and a harrowing awareness of their limited prospects – and the closing note of muted affirmation has been earned by not eliding the pain that has preceded it.

A different take on the Aborigine in Australian society emerges from Amiel Courtin-Wilson's documentary, seven years in the making, which chronicles the life of Jack Charles, who founded an Aboriginal theatre company when he wasn't otherwise engaged as a cat burglar. Jack talks most of the time, as the film slips between different periods, and very engagingly,

Sample page from Australian Book Review, Dec 2009–Jan 2010

With film reviewing, the whole business of 'going to the pictures' has changed. For some decades now, I've gone equipped with clipboard, paper and biro at the ready, and spend a lot of time scribbling sometimes-indecipherable notes in the dark. As I'm not a daily newspaper reviewer, though on several occasions in the 90s I stood in as *The Sunday Age* critic when friend Tom Ryan was on leave, my deadlines are usually less pressing, and this means I can often see the film a second time or follow up a preview screening with a DVD-viewing at home. Since the film writing I'm involved in (e.g., for *Metro* magazine or, over six years, as film critic for *Meanjin*) usually requires about three times the length of the average newspaper review, there's the scope — and need — for more detail of a kind that you can't always pick up in a single viewing. *Metro* most often wants reviews of new Australian films and is generous about space, and its production design makes one *look* good. Recently I've been asked by *Metro* to cover Baz Luhrmann's semi-dumb *Australia* and the film version of J.M. Coetzee's masterly novel *Disgrace*, but the very amiable editor Peter Tapp has been amenable to other suggestions as well. For instance, I had the chance to compare the film of Alan Bennett's *The History Boys* with those other history boys in the (essentially idiotic) *300*; and to expose my latent nastiness in a piece called 'A curmudgeon's canon' in which I explained my preference for such cringe-television programmes as *The Office* and *Summer Heights High*. And since early 2007, *Metro* has been paying me a retainer to edit a series of definitive research essays on Australian films of the 70s and 80s for which new prints had been struck, and the aim is now to reproduce the first twelve in book form as they seem to have a permanent usefulness in the thoroughness of their research.

Not all reviewing involves writing, however. For several years in the early 1990s, I did regular monthly spots with compère Derek Guiles for ABC Regional, where the challenge was to manage to say something worthwhile about two or three films in the twenty-minute time slot, and from late 1996 to the present day I've done usually two, sometimes three, monthly programmes on Radio 3RRR's *Film Buff's Forecast*. Its producer Paul Harris has usually given me a choice of what films I elect

Beyond the cringe: tricky Ricky and *The Office*

If Ricky Gervais' *The Office* didn't actually introduce the idea of cringe television, it is by now perhaps the program most closely associated with the mode. Steve Coogan's naff reporter Alan Partridge is as wholly self-centred and as unaware as David Brent of the impression he makes on other people; and Chris Langham as Roy Mallard in *People Like Us*, with his roving mic, is terminally and embarrassingly inept. But Partridge is not quite as crudely self-seeking as Gervais' David Brent, and Mallard keeps stumbling over his own efforts to be self-effacing. Australia's Wayne Hope, in his Don Angel persona in *Very Small Business*, has to keep slipping around to maintain some control over his life, and this is probably also the case with his *Stupid Stupid Man* character, Carl Van Dyke, whose sexism is encapsulated in his casual remark to his secretary 'G'day sweetie, make us a cup of coffee, would you, love?' One might make the odd excuse for any of these as they go on their blinkered way, but with Brent it is as painful as it is funny to watch as he puts his foot wrong every time, without ever being aware of it.

A local television reviewer, writing about the American version of *The Office*, noted:

Like that other US adaptation (you know the one [i.e., Kath & Kim]) this is broader, softer and much prettier than the original. But in this case, that's no bad thing. The British original, for all its brilliance, was so excruciating you regularly had to leave the room.[3]

Well, there's an element of hyperbole in that, but it is true that David Brent is possibly the least likeable protagonist of any television series in living memory – and the one you can least easily take your eyes off. He can't talk on the phone without rolling his eyes to anyone watching, to suggest what a cool dude he is. His casual and inveterate racism reaches its apotheosis in his 'joke' in which he asks, 'What's black and slides down Nelson's Column?' My delicate liberal sensitivities forbid my giving you the answer. When it is decided that the Swindon branch of the paper manufacturing company should take over the Slough office where Brent has reigned supreme, he does his best to undermine the process, torn between competing with the incoming Swindon boss, Neil, (even to the point of buying – and badly wearing – the same leather blouson) and bad-mouthing him to the Slough staff, of whose loyalty Brent is fatuously and erroneously sure.

From 'A curmudgeon's canon', Metro, No. 160, 2009, pp 134-38

to review, though I maintain that he has sent me off to see some of the very worst movies of recent years, such as the unspeakable Rimbaud biopic, *Total Eclipse*, and the lugubrious talk-fest, *Winter Guest*. One of the challenges in this reviewing has been warding off when possible Paul's appalling puns. They are actually sometimes quite clever, but I wouldn't want him to know this. One of the rewards is that he shares my enthusiasm for British cinema and is always happy to have me talk about — and up — the newest film from, say, Michael Winterbottom or Mike Leigh, or much more esoteric numbers like *Two Men Went to War* or *Wondrous Oblivion* which had to be tracked down in the suburbs.

He is also willing to have new books on British cinema reviewed (and to interview me about my own — the sales, of course, soar as a result), and likes to have tributes paid to the recently dead collaborators in our favourite national cinema. What is more surprising is the steady trickle — it would be boastful to call it a stream — of responses we get from the listening audience, reassuring us that not everyone is obsessed with the latest exploits of Spiderman or Batman. And one listener, with a passion for 1930s British cinema, has generously plied me with videos and DVDs of rare movies of that period, thereby filling gaps in my insatiable need to know all about this Hollywood *manqué*, as some would say, or a viable alternative, as *I* would.

Meanjin, Australia's oldest literary journal, gave me a chance to pull together fifty-odd years of film-going in the interests of writing a quarterly account of a selection of new films. It was edited for six distinguished years by Ian Britain whom I'd first taught in Year 9 French at Trinity Grammar School, and thirty years later had recruited to teach the novel-to-film course I was running at Monash. Roles were reversed when he asked me to be *Meanjin*'s critic, imposing no conditions except that the pieces were to be not more than about 4000 words and, if possible, to have some connection with the over-all theme of any particular issue. For instance, in a 2005 issue subtitled 'Portraits of the Artist', I could draw on *A Song to Remember* (always good to keep Merle Oberon's name before the public) and the 1945 airbrushing of Cole Porter's life, *Night and Day*, as well as an assortment of biopics about writers including *Julia* (with Jason Robards's Dashiell Hammett smoking himself silly as he typed away) and Joseph Strick's adventurous 1977 filming of Joyce's *A Portrait of the Artist as a Young Man*, painters such as *Pollock* (2002), with Ed Harris sloshing paint over a large area of canvas, and singers (Larry Parks's famous black-face turn in *The Jolson Story*, 1946). All this was by way of leading into, and interspersed with, more extended accounts of appropriate films of the quarter: *De-Lovely*, a more candid go at Porter's life; Colin Firth and Scarlett Johansson bringing to life Vermeer's *Girl with a Pearl Earring*; *Stage Beauty*, Richard

'What had always interested me about this story ... was the contrast between the public perception of the Queen – a dour, stout figure in black with an expression of permanent disapproval – and the strong-willed, passionate, romantic girl she had been when she came to the throne in 1837.'

– SCREENWRITER JULIAN FELLOWES

record – Victoria is referred to at the end of the new film as 'the longest-reigning sovereign to date'. Which brings me at last to *The Young Victoria* – according to one source, the ninety-fifth big- or small-screen appearance (since silent days) of this most durable monarch.'

Victoria on the screen

If royalty in general has exercised filmmakers' craft and imagination, Victoria appears to have held a special fascination for them. In the 1930s, Anna Neagle famously appeared twice as Victoria.[2] The first time was in *Victoria the Great* (Herbert Wilcox, 1937), a film that may be seen to reinforce the role of the monarchy in the troubling wake of Edward VIII's abdication, with the film 'celebrat[ing] a perfect marriage and a dedicated partnership in the service of the nation'.[3] Following the success of this film, *Sixty Glorious Years* (Herbert Wilcox, 1938) appeared the next year, dealing with the latter part of Victoria's life, perhaps extolling national unity in the face of the war clouds gathering over Europe, asserting 'the need to protect Britain's national security',[4] Neagle's is a very ladylike monarch; this is an image one now sees as belonging to an earlier period when royalty was less exposed to the public gaze and to criticism.

British royals in (mainly) British films

There isn't space here to do justice to the screen representation of monarchies. Leaving Victoria to one side for the moment, just think of this royal parade down the ages: the charismatic young Peter O'Toole doing a brilliant turn as Henry II, and his contentious queen, Eleanor, making a star entrance from a barge in the person of the quarter-century older Katharine Hepburn in *The Lion in Winter* (Anthony Harvey, 1968); Laurence Olivier, via Shakespeare, calling Englishmen to rally to the nation's defence in a World War II version of *Henry V* (Laurence Olivier, 1944) and Kenneth Branagh striking a different pose in his 1989 film for the same king from the same play; Charles Laughton stomping about studio sets in Holbein postures in *The Private Life of Henry VIII* (Alexander Korda, 1933), which incidentally was the first British film to break substantially into the American mainstream markets; and Henry VIII's daughter, eponymously played by Cate Blanchett in *Elizabeth* (Shekhar Kapur, 1998) and in its (dire) sequel *Elizabeth: The Golden Age* (Shekhar Kapur, 2007), as well as by Flora Robson in *Fire Over England* (William K. Howard, 1937) and *The Sea Hawk* (Michael Curtiz, 1940), and by Glenda Jackson, who'd 'done' Elizabeth memorably

on TV, doing her again on the big screen and crossing verbal swords with Vanessa Redgrave in *Mary Queen of Scots* (Charles Jarrott, 1971).

The list goes on and on, without even touching on American attempts at interpreting British royalty, such as 'Queen' Bette Davis, frizzled and later bald, in *The Private Lives of Elizabeth and Essex* (Michael Curtiz, 1939). Before *The Young Victoria* (Jean-Marc Vallée, 2009), one of the most recent and perhaps most distinguished of all the 'royal' films, there was Stephen Frears' unambiguously titled *The Queen* (2006), which enshrined Helen Mirren's uncanny and touching portrayal of Elizabeth II, who needs to reign a few more years to pass Victoria's

There was plenty of criticism in Britain over the importation of US star Irene Dunne to play the ageing queen brought out of seclusion by (fanciful) dealings in *The Mudlark* (Jean Negulesco, 1950). Presumably this casting was for US box-office reasons, as there were plenty of British actresses whose cheeks could just as convincingly been puffed out with cotton wool. There were sketches of Victoria by, among many others, Fay Compton in *The Prime Minister* (Thorold Dickinson, 1941),

From 'Royal Parade: The Young Victoria *and others'*
Metro, No. 163, 2009

Eyre's fascinating take on a crucial period in the life of Restoration actor, 'Ned' Kynaston, unnecessarily played by minor US actor Billy Crudup when there were plenty of British actors who could have done it better; *Finding Neverland*, with Johnny Depp doing his best to bring J.M. Barrie to screen life (you'd think there were no British actors who could play these roles. Oh, I know about US box-office demands); and Nathaniel Khan's wonderful evocation of his father Louis in the documentary *My Architect*.

In recent months, filmgoers have been made privy to the privacies and privations of painter Vermeer (*Girl with a Pearl Earring*), poet Sylvia Plath (*Sylvia*), composer Porter, again (*De-Lovely*), architect Louis Khan (*My Architect*), actor Edward Kynaston (*Stage Beauty*) and playwright James Barrie (*Finding Neverland*). If none of these offers the banalities of *A Song to Remember*, they are not without their own moments of cliché and sentimentality. Writers are perhaps the most difficult of all to render in cinematically interesting form as they go about their art. Joseph Strick's brave 1977 version of James Joyce's *A Portrait of the Artist as a Young Man* avoided the stereotypical shots of the author looking glum or obsessed over his quill or type-writer or computer (think of Jason Robards smoking himself silly as Dashiell Hammett as he typed away in *Julia*, 1977) by focusing, as Joyce does, on the forma-tive influences that will shape the potential artist. He allows protagonist Stephen Dedalus to talk at length about how he must use and/or put behind him the expe-riences of his first twenty years, and the film stops at his neophyte steps as author.

More often sources of the artist's genesis and development are rather cursorily dealt with. How did a nice American girl like Sylvia Plath end up writing tormented verse in rainy England prior to killing herself? What has brought the marriage of J.M. Barrie to the pass seen at the start of *Neverland*? How important was Porter's ambivalent sexuality to his growth as man and artist? How does Edward Kynaston's sexuality inform his pre-eminence as a portrayer of women on the Restoration stage? All right, none of these films is offered as a full-scale life of the artist, and given the scope of a two- to three-hour film as compared with, say, a 400-page biography, it would be unreasonable to expect a like concern for the minutiae that we expect of a written work. Nevertheless, sometimes it would add depth to the biopic to be given more sense of where the creative inspiration and activity have come from.

From 'Portraits in Celluloid', Meanjin, 2005, Vol 64

In a 2006 issue subtitled 'Cosmopolis', under the heading 'Leaving Manhattan', I was able to show some connection with the journal's city theme while writing about two seemingly disparate films. These were Bennett Miller's *Capote* and Woody Allen's *Match Point*: the first, in Philip Seymour Hoffman's brilliant incarnation of Truman Capote, out of his gossipy New York territory as he chronicles a mass-murder in Kansas; the second, Allen as director, perhaps not wholly wisely or successfully, forsaking his home-ground for a touristy view of London. The journal's themes were always broad enough to accommodate (with only moderate manoeuvring) a batch of films I wanted to write about — trailing in their wake memories of a past so much of which had been spent in darkened cinemas. There was a real sense of luxury in being able to write at some length and to have enough lead-in time to think about connections among the films new and old — and probably an element of self-indulgence as well. Under the Britain regime, the *Meanjin* office was the untidiest I have ever seen, but Ian claimed to know where everything was and the precision and insight of his editing skills, always strikingly at odds with the surrounding chaos, forced me to believe him.

One of the things I really want to boast about is that in 1992 I became a touch typist, and without this skill I doubt if I could have undertaken all the writing jobs I have — and plan to go on with. But don't think it was easy. From the end of the academic teaching year in early November 1991 to the start of the next in March the following year, I persevered for an hour every day with a computer programme enticingly called 'Touch', which promised me the skill implied in its name. The real spur to success was the fact that every time you made a mistake on this programme a bell rang through the house and, as there were quite a few people coming and going over that summer period, the place rang with the bell-sound and the callous laughter of the other occupants. The humiliation was so great that my progress was faster than I feel it might have been in more caring circumstances. It was in any case an immense time-saver: there was no longer the need to approach over-burdened secretaries with the scrawled results of my thinking, then to check their efforts and return the script for corrections. In fact, learning to type (when I was young, only girls were taught this at school, as if we chaps would always be in superior positions with female minions to do our bidding) and to operate a computer have been crucial in serving my writing compulsiveness. One by-product is that my hand-writing, never stylish but once at least legible, now defies my own interpretation. I wonder if those 'recent university studies' which can prove anything they set their minds to may find a connection between computer skills and the decline of the written hand.

In late 1997, Neil Sinyard, a friend at the University of Hull offered me the only bribe which I've ever had that wasn't an insult to my integrity. Would I like to co-edit with him a series of monographs on British Film Makers that he was proposing to Manchester University Press? 'You could do one on Lance Comfort,' he added slyly, and that's what I mean by an irresistible bribe. How could I turn down a chance to bring to world-wide attention my hero whose *Great Day* had so long ago inducted me into the beauties of British cinema? In the event, the book on Comfort began the series which now comprises twenty titles which regularly sell to small but satisfied audiences — 'fit but few' as Milton said about the possible reading public for *Paradise Lost*. Anyway, I immersed myself in my Comfort zone, and after the wide-ranging researches required by the *Oxford Companion to Australian Film*, it was very rewarding to focus on a single, if prolific, filmmaker and to try to sort out (convincingly, as far as readers would be concerned) why I'd so much admired a filmmaker who had never seemed to me to be adequately appreciated. His production manager son, John Comfort, and John's film-accountant wife Maureen, were hospitable and helpful in all sorts of ways. I think John was glad that his father might at last get some recognition, and he must have been even more pleased when the National Film Theatre, London, in August 2008, ran a short sell-out season of Lance's films to mark his centenary.

The researches for this book involved first, and most enjoyably, watching repeatedly as many of Comfort's films as possible. The archive located in the bowels of the British Film Institute yielded such rarities as the charming piece of Victoriana, the film version of J.B. Priestley's *When We Are Married,* and the masterly *noir* melodrama, *Temptation Harbour,* derived from a novel by Georges Simenon and certainly one of the most 'French-looking' films ever made in Britain. Why no one has transferred this to DVD is a major mystery, especially now that several other Comfort pieces are so available. Sources in the UK and the US brought other missing titles my way, including *Bang! You're Dead,* an unsettling look at the shabbiness left in the wake of World War Two, and the riveting kidnap thriller *Tomorrow at Ten.* Like several other British filmmakers who had done more prestigious work in the 1940s but were out of step with the main trends of the 50s, Comfort turned to making 'B' films, the movies designed for the bottom half of the double-bill, which was the standard exhibition practice of the period. Unlike those others though (e.g., Bernard Knowles, Arthur Crabtree, etc), he seemed invigorated by the unforgiving schedules and parsimonious budgets of the 'B'-movie business and responded with crisp, compelling narratives that are so much more watchable than many of the posher products of the decade. The research also included talking to as many of his collaborators as I could run to earth, and invariably they held to the view that 'He was such a nice man'. Perhaps he needed to be more ruthless to survive at the higher level of filmmaking in which he'd made his name in the 40s, but, equally, he never put his name to any rubbish, to any film of which he needed to feel ashamed.

At the end of the previous chapter I introduced the word 'encyclopedia' in relation to British film, suggesting how the preparation for the interviews would have been greatly speeded up by a single, reliable reference work. Lack of this meant that I was always dodging around checking information in this or that biography or studio history ... whatever, as the young now so mindlessly say. Anyway, with the backing of the very nice publisher then at Methuen, Michael

Early, I applied for and got a grant to support this enterprise. Applying for grants from the Australian government was, like marriage, not to be undertaken lightly or ill-advisedly. The process of getting the application together took most of January 1998, and when I showed what I'd prepared to the Dean of the Monash Arts Faculty he said, 'It sounds a bit like a retirement project, Brian.' 'It is,' I said. 'I know, but it mustn't sound like one,' was his shrewd reply. With his help, the application was adjusted to sound less pleasurable and, further, he'd said, 'You're not asking for enough money,' so we found ways to adjust the sum asked for. In the last phone conversation I had with my father before he died in December of that year, he was stunned to hear that I'd been awarded a six-figure grant to produce the *Encyclopedia*. Dad had never really come to terms with the idea that you might be paid to go to the movies and then write about them, let alone get what was to him a large sum of money for the purpose, but he was impressed with the news.

The letter announcing this grant, without which I couldn't have contemplated the enterprise, said: 'Your contribution to the creation of knowledge is of critical importance to Australia as we head towards the twenty-first century'. 'Oh,' said my wife. 'How?' Of course, if I'd had any real integrity I would have turned it down as I was not in sympathy with the government at this time. However, the grant and top-ups from Monash University enabled me to employ a brilliant research assistant for over three years — a former student of mine, Melinda Hildebrandt, then embarking on a PhD on British cinema. On rare occasions when she needed time off (e.g., to get on with her own thesis), my rate of progress was halved. My only complaint about her had to do with two newish actresses I was taken with and was determined to include entries on. Of one, Melinda, echoing the response these two women had evoked in my own home, said, 'I think we need to have a little chat about her.' And of the other, 'Perhaps we should talk about her again in a year's time and see if she's done anything interesting by then.' They are of course included, and rightly so, but their names are not to be disclosed here.

175

By contrast with the highly focussed research for the Lance Comfort book, this was to be both wide-ranging and, I suppose, relatively superficial. The first stage was the choosing of the 'headwords' — that is, the people, companies, themes and so on that were to receive individual entries — and this process occupied every Friday of the first year of the project. There were about 5,800 entries in the first edition and that has now been increased so that the fourth edition will have over 500 more than the first. A very early decision had to be made as to whether we would concentrate on longer essays on major figures, institutions, etc, or shorter pieces on a wider range. Quite quickly I decided to aim for less about more rather than more about less (or fewer, to be grammatical). My argument for this was that if you didn't know all you wanted to know about, say, Sean Connery or David Lean or Hammer Studios, then that, essentially, was your fault, because there were already plenty of places in which you could have found it out. I don't mean that there wasn't scope for further appraisals of such major figures and topics, only that it seemed more important to bring to attention as well the many others who seldom make it into reference books. I had in mind a wide range of behind-camera personnel (cinematographers, editors, production and costume designers, composers and music directors, sound recordists, casting directors and continuity 'girls' as they used to be called) as well as hundreds of those imperishable and prolific character actors who have been one of the enduring glories of British film. I don't meant that Connery et al weren't going to get the substantial entries their pre-eminence would suggest; it was just that I was equally concerned to do justice to the likes of toothy Joyce Grenfell with her rallying approach to life's vicissitudes, or Raymond Huntley, archetypal bureaucratic sourpuss, or music directors such as Muir Mathieson, who may just have the most credits of anyone in British film.

Obviously, choosing these subjects for entry couldn't be rushed, and wasn't. I started by using the standard international works such as Halliwell's Who's Who in the Movies and Ephraim Katz's The

Film Encyclopedia, on the understanding that any British personnel or company that turned up in these non-specialist works would certainly have to be included in a volume wholly devoted to British cinema. And this same principle was applied to a couple of general film reference books of the 1930s for guidance on personnel prolific perhaps in that earlier period but more or less forgotten in recent decades. We then scoured works of increasing specialisation. These included such titles as John Huntley's *British Film Music*, with its valuable 'Biographical Index', Duncan Petrie's *The British Cinematographer*, Edward Carrick's *Art Design in the British Film*, Marcia Landy's *British Genres: Cinema and Society* (1930-1960) — dozens, perhaps hundreds more, before the list of headwords was in place. When I say 'in place', don't imagine it was by any means fixed. It was a working-list on which to begin writing entries, but we kept adding to this list almost up to the time of sending off the manuscript to the publisher. People kept suggesting smart new names or old ones they feared I might have overlooked — and they have continued to do so, so that, as I said, the second and third editions between them have yielded a further 400 entries. As to getting rid of names I'd thought promising when doing the first three editions but who have subsequently seemed not able to get projects off the ground, I've so far not removed any: it just seems too callous. Why, I can't but wonder, has John Furse not followed up the brilliant hostage thriller, *Blind Flight*, made in 2002? Or why has it taken Jamie Thraves, director of the very endearing 2000 film, *The Low-Down*, nine years to make his next feature, *Cry of the Owl*? In both cases, they had done work so impressive that I wanted their entries to stay in place.

But it wasn't just a matter of 'names'. I was planning an *Encyclopedia*, not a *Who's Who*, though inevitably there would be a strong element of the latter in it, and of course the biographical entries quickly asserted at least numerical supremacy. However, the aim was to spread the net as widely as possible to include all the major companies and studios and a good many minor ones (Patricia Warren's *British Film Studios* was indispensable for these), organisations associated with the conduct of British cinema, both as a cultural force and as an industry (the BFI's annual *Film and Television Handbooks* had useful lists), and other specialist books like Margaret Dickinson and Sarah Street's *Cinema and State*, and Allan Foster's *The Movie Traveller* (about filming locations in Britain), to choose two at random, provided information relevant to particular entries. By such entries, I mean short thematic entries on such aspects of filmmaking as 'legislation', 'finance', 'exhibition' and 'locations'. These thematic entries were perhaps the hardest to finalise. I kept thinking: It would be good to have one on (for example) 'London on film' or 'village life' or 'episodic films' or 'coal-mining in British cinema' and many more such wildly assorted topics. The danger with this, when we moved beyond proper names, was the choice might begin to look a bit eccentric, but that seemed a risk worth taking.

Actually, I didn't want it to be 'eccentric', but I did want the whole thing to have a flavour. It wasn't to be just a list of credits, for instance. You can find those quite easily, especially now with websites (of varying reliability) devoted to such information. If I was to be writing about actors, I wanted, in the necessarily limited space, to give a sense of their qualities and of their careers. This seemed especially important in the case of character actors whose typical film personas might have been better known than their names. It also meant that opinions crept in: nothing too wildly idiosyncratic, which might have undermined the book's value as a reference work, but enough to give the book some flavour. Also, frankly, it had to be fun to do. It was taking the last years of my middle age and I wasn't out to be bored.

I think, though, I must be rather thick. It kept being borne in on me that this was turning into a big job. You'd think the word 'encyclopedia' in the title would have alerted me to this. I remember when my daughter Susannah, then aged about ten, was deeply immersed in *The Budgerigar Owner's Encyclopedia*, and even that was a substantial work, though some of its entries seemed to me terse to the point of brutality. For example, under 'Heart Attack', it simply said 'The first sign of a heart attack in a budgerigar is its sudden death', with no suggestion of "Try the peck of life". I can't remember at exactly what stage it became apparent to me that I wasn't going to be able to write the whole thing myself, much as I'd have liked to. However, common sense prevailed over unbridled egoism and I sent off letters of invitation to well over a hundred people in three continents and was pleased with the high level of acceptance. There were obviously going to be areas that needed specialised knowledge as distinct from being cobbled together by me who hadn't got that specialised knowledge of, say, the documentary movement or sound or propaganda or religion in British film. As far as possible these entries were earmarked for experts in the particular field: so, to choose a few at random, David Burnand, Head of the Centre for Film Music at the Royal College of Music, did three major entries on classical music, original scores and popular music in British films; the entries on J. Arthur Rank and the Rank Organisation were written by Rank's biographer, Geoffrey Macnab; Charles Barr wrote on Ealing Studios; Andrew Spicer, author of *Typical Men*, did the British male stars entry; Cathy Surowiec, author of *Accent on Design*, wrote the entry on 'costume design', Kevin Brownlow 'did' David Lean in 800 words, as distinct from the 800 *pages* of his famous biography; and the piece on 'continuity' was the work of one of the industry's most respected practitioners, Elaine Schreyeck. By the time of the fourth edition, there are over 120 authors who were responsible for the nearly 200,000 words I reluctantly let go, content- ing myself with the remaining 700,000.

With the Headwords and authors tentatively in place, I addressed the task of writing the unallocated entries, about 5000 of them, and the task proved almost entirely enjoyable. If one is more accustomed to arguing one's way through whole books or chapters of books or academic articles, there is something remarkably satisfying about writing, say, a dozen short pieces over a couple of days. It's again the finiteness of the task that's a refreshing change: the word limit for each of these entries could be constraining, but one knew that it would be finished by lunchtime, as it were. Having opted for the less-about-more approach, the challenge was then to bring actors, directors and so on to life in a few hundred words. The aim was, in the biographical entries, to give a sense of the career trajectory of the personality involved: this meant being as concise as possible about biographical facts and leaving enough room to vivify the actual film contribution each had made. From this point of view, I think doing the entries on the character players was my greatest pleasure: in the history of British cinema, the star system may never have been as firmly established as it was in Hollywood, but there was no doubting its depth of character acting. My aim was to give some sense of the pleasure to be had from the likes of Michael Balfour, invariably shifty, or John Horsley, who may have arrested on film more felons than any cop in real life.

There was no hard and fast criterion for inclusion. As a rough working rule-of-thumb, I decided that, for individuals, they should have been involved in at least five British films. But I felt it would be wrong to exclude such celebrated figures from British theatre as Marie Tempest or Gwen Ffrangçon-Davies or Tyrone Guthrie because they'd thoughtlessly failed to come up with five titles. The fact that they'd been caught on celluloid at all was occasion enough to include such people so distinguished in their own fields that their venture into film was worth noting. Then there was the matter of visitors to Britain. Tim Bergfelder, expert on European émigrés in British film, suggested many who should be included, and, better still, offered to write the pieces on them. But what of those US actors (and, occasionally, directors) who prolonged their careers — if not their reputations — in Britain, particularly in the 1950s? Wouldn't it be worth recording the presences here of such monstresses as Bette Davis and Joan Crawford in British horror films? Or all those square-jawed chaps, like Dane Clark and Lee Patterson, who in the 1950s showed the British police how to round up a gang of low-lifes? They were part of the scene during a prolific decade or so, and, in my view, they needed to be included.

As for finding reliable information about this vast cast of characters, one could rely up to a point on such data bases as the Internet Movie Data Base (imdb), but I found I was also using a wide range of sources. These included various editions of *Who's Who in the Theatre,* Peter Noble's *British Film and Television Yearbooks* (embracing decades from the post-war years until the 1980s), and the BFI's *British Television,* because there was no point in ignoring the fact that, for British actors to survive in their chosen profession, most needed to find niches of various kinds in TV as well as in film (and the theatre too if possible). One of the chief difficulties was in ascertaining exactly where and, especially, *when* participants had been born. Some actors, particularly, had been famously creative in regard to this basic information, and one sees why an actress of a certain (= uncertain) age might want to knock off a few years, but when it comes to preparing a standard work like an *Encyclopedia* it seemed to me that there wasn't room for gallantry in this matter. To this end, I had marvellous support from a mole in the British Film Institute, Janice Healey, who used to visit the Family Record Office regularly and would email me her findings every Sunday. With her help, we laid to rest the widely disseminated untruth that director Leslie Arliss was the son of silent and early-talkie star, George Arliss, and that Leslie had become keen on the movies while in Hollywood with his dad, George, in the 1920s. For £20, we bought Leslie's birth certificate, which proved that Leslie's father worked for the gas company and was unlikely to have been in Hollywood with young Leslie in the 20s. As well, my research assistant and I sent off over 200 letters to people impertinently asking when and where they were born, and trying to soften the impertinence by requesting other less controversial information. To my astonishment, we had over 150 replies to these requests. On occasion, several even rang me at home at improbable (Australian) hours to give me the information I was after.

Apart from the biographical entries, there were hundreds of others on matters connected with British film, as industry or art form, and in writing these one's own sense of the general contours would need to be checked against those specialist writers who'd done such valiant spade-work. Much of the research in compiling a book like *The Encyclopedia of British Film* is secondary in nature: you are dependent on the primary research of myriad others who have investigated, for instance, the history of British studios or of the ways in which British film has sought to finance itself over the decades. Or of the rich but comparatively recently excavated history of the British silent film. I knew my grasp of this would be no more than tenuous, which was why I sought an associate editor in Anthony Slide, an acknowledged authority on silent film.

Because of the magnitude of the undertaking, and because, being an Australian and *in* Australia for the duration of the project, apart from visits to England to do accumulated researches at the BFI, I asked the publishers to appoint three vetters. These three read everything I and the authors wrote and made invaluable suggestions, for instance, in relation to plugging gaps in my knowledge of acting careers on television or the stage. I'd seen a lot of British television and had long been fascinated with British theatre, but from the other side of the world I couldn't be sure I hadn't overlooked some significant credit that should be included to hint at the wider career involved. The vetters were also able to ensure that my information about institutions and companies was up to date, that I hadn't overlooked some major shift in power. They would also curb me on occasion when what I had said might have been construed as offensive or even litigious, as on the occasion when I described an actress as having married a noted hell-raiser and divorced him in short order 'as one would have to'. As well, I had two well-placed friends in Australia who also read every word, and would give me back annotations on, say, the letter M with marginal queries like, 'Are you sure this is what you mean to say?'

There were infinite difficulties — at least, they seemed infinite at the time — in pinning down release dates, in ensuring that all the collaborating countries were listed after a film title. I think that, if I were doing it again from scratch (appalling thought), I wouldn't bother about this latter and would just indicate that every film to which no list of countries involved is attached has some significant British input. The problem of deciding what is a British film grows ever more complex: we've come a long way from the days when a British film was one starring Dirk Bogarde and was made at Pinewood. You knew where you were then; or at least you knew where *they* were.

The *EBF* was finally launched in London in September 2003 by Jean Kent, and to a very rousing reception from a crowd that included such cross-the-decades representatives of British film as Sydney Samuelson, Muriel Pavlow, Roy Ward Baker, Rita Tushingham, Bryan Forbes and Stephen Frears. In Sydney it was launched by the wonderfully durable screen and stage partnership of Googie Withers and John McCallum, with Michael Craig and 1940s musical comedy star Carol Raye also present, and in Melbourne by Miriam Margolyes, standing in for Geoffrey Rush who'd been called to Los Angeles. When it came to reception, I felt I could have prepared a pro forma for reviewers, to save them the trouble of asking crossly, 'By what possible criteria has McFarlane included so-and-so and excluded the equally distinguished or minor figure B?' In the event, the book had an easier critical run than I'd expected. It was generally received as filling a gap, which was my stated aim in the opening sentence of the Introduction, and on the whole people seemed not to object to its somewhat idiosyncratic tone. I mean, I never wanted it to be a mere matter of lists of films and companies and organisations: I wanted it to have a critical edge and, if that meant it was sometimes seen as 'irreverent' as one critic said, that was all right by me. The one exception I remember from its kindly critical reception was from a Moscow-based online correspondent quoted by Amazon who described it as 'a tragic misfire'. This person seemed to want more juicy detail about the private lives in the biographical entries whereas I'd mistakenly chosen to concentrate on the films. I was reminded of being in London when the great Beatrice Lillie played *Auntie*

Mame on stage in 1958. Placards around the foyer of the Adelphi Theatre said things like 'A wow and a winner' and 'Hilarious from start to finish'. In the middle, in front of the box-office, one placard said: '"A total disaster" Harold Hobson, *Sunday Times*' and next to it was another placard simply stating 'HOUSE FULL'. I liked the idea of using 'a tragic misfire' on the cover of the third edition, but it seemed a bit smartypants and might have discouraged sales.

As well as critical reaction, I've had comments from a wide range of individuals, some more useful than others. I'd included an email address and in any case my Monash affiliation was easy enough to trace, while yet others had at me via the publisher. There are those who find it a handy adjunct to viewing films on television and wrote to say so, along with those who sent me corrections (often replete with exclamation marks implying 'I can't believe such ignorance!' or 'She died in the Cotswolds!') and I'm grateful to these. There are even a few personally outraged that I hadn't adequately valued, say, their father's work or their own. 'My father never made a 'B' movie in his life!' emailed one seething but misinformed daughter, whose outrage did more credit to her filial devotion than to her aesthetic judgment. I decided simply to be very brave about this kind of thing, having in mind my personal definition of a reference book as 'a long work containing some errors.' And in subsequent editions these have been amended: if you embark on compiling an encyclopedia in an area where there has not been so all-embracing a work before, it seemed to me you had to risk getting some things wrong, and to hope that people would draw attention to these as they have.

Since this vast and time-consuming project, I've continued reviewing, co-authored (with Monash colleague Deane Williams) a book on the prolific director Michael Winterbottom, and researched a monograph on screen adaptations of *Great Expectations*. This latter proved a fascinating exercise for the way in which the original plan — to study David Lean's adaptation in relation to the novel — kept ballooning out. It became apparent as I came across more and more kinds of adaptation and extrapolation from Dickens's original (stage and radio versions, novels derived from it, even a children's animated movie, as well as many television and film versions) that there is something about this text that keeps it relevant and important to large numbers of people in succeeding decades.

The longest-running project overlapping these just named has been a book on the British 'B'movie, co-authored with British colleague Steve Chibnall. Only filmgoers with long memories will remember the days when you got two films (plus newsreel, cartoon etc) for your money. There would be an interval between the 'supporting' or 'B' film and the main feature, and if you were a young man taking a girl (or 'young woman' as they came to be called when feminism got under way) it was hideously expensive for you. Fresh (mostly) from the 'B'movie, you'd push your way into the foyer where you'd be expected to ply her with expensive groceries: chocolates, drinks, ice creams. There was no end to it. And it's not as if they'd paid their share of the tickets either, or fares or, if you were trying to be really impressive, taxis. I know all this has probably changed today. Young men today have no idea of the privations of their elders. Where, I ask, were the feminists when I needed them?

However, this bitter personal recollection is really to one side of the main point at issue. Whereas the Hollywood 'B'movie had had at least one distinguished champion in James Agee and several such American second features as Edgar Ulmer's *Detour* or any of the 1940s Val Lewton horror films for RKO, including *Cat People* or *I Walked with a Zombie,* had deservedly acquired cult status, this had not been the case with the British 'B'film. Perhaps it was a matter of reflected obloquy deriving from the scorn, not always warranted, that had been poured upon the 'quota quickies' of the 1930s, films often made in a hurry for improbably low budgets. Such supporting films dwindled during the war years, but returned to enjoy their period of greatest prolificacy in the 1950s and 60s, and in hindsight were often much more entertaining than their critical dismissal at the time might have led you to suppose. Steve and I were interested in pursuing their history, their reception, what they suggested about

185

widely held mores of the time and just how intrinsically interesting they were. With this in mind, I viewed somewhere between three and four hundred of them and I came to revise my opinions considerably. Back in 1996 when I was preparing an article on them for a US journal, I watched no more than about sixty or seventy, but enough to lead Gerie, who would be half-watching while cutting up vegetables or ironing, to say at one point: 'Look, am I right in thinking that these films are all about a guy in a trench coat prowling round in the dark and the rain trying to save a young woman with a nice perm, New Look clothes and refined vowels from a dangerous situation she needn't have been in? As a result she's taking up time he should be spending in rounding up criminals with common or foreign accents?' 'Yes, that's right,' I answered carelessly before I'd begun to see the more diverse merits of these neglected films. The best are probably such taut thrillers as *Cash on Demand*, starring Peter 'Frankenstein' Cushing, and *Strongroom*, but there are also the odd charming comedy such as *The Man Who Liked Funerals* and the rare socially responsible drama like *Private Information*, starring my old friend Jill Esmond. No, these British 'B's can no longer be lightly written off and their increasing availability on DVD means they don't need to be. *The British 'B' Film* was launched at the National Film Theatre in London in December 2009, in the presence of Rona Anderson, unquestioned 'Queen of the 'B's', and hardly seeming a day older than when she was doing all those plucky things from which she had to be rescued by the likes of Dermot Walsh. These two are on the cover, and from the position of Dermot's hands it is unclear whether it is passion or strangulation he has in mind for Rona.

Virtually everything relating to a lifetime's obsession with films and with writing about them has been pure pleasure. That includes DVD liners which offer the challenge of saying something useful, without perjuring one's immortal soul, about such diverse titles as *The Cars that Ate Paris*, *Lord of the Flies* and Joseph Losey's *La Truite*. This is a quite demanding kind of writing: it's got to be both academically respectable and at the same time accessible and interesting to a prospective readership well beyond academe. More recently, I've been asked to do voice-overs for DVDs of such British classics as *Pygmalion* and *The Browning Version*. People are willing, it seems, to watch a film on DVD, then watch it again with the sound turned down while they listen to my voice telling them what they should have been observing if they'd known what to look for. As well, there is acute pleasure in the intensive research needed to do entries on British film notables for the *Oxford Dictionary of National Biography*. The aim, in a thousand or so words, is to do justice to the likes of John Mills, Margaretta Scott, Kay Walsh, John Schlesinger, Michael Relph, Marius Goring and Leslie Norman, all of whom I'd met and could thus draw on personal impressions as well as recorded data. One whom I 'did' but sadly hadn't met was the exquisite Anna Lee, star of British films in the 1930s before going to, and staying in, Hollywood; and others included the impresario Lord Delfont, lovely Sally Gray of the eloquent voice and slightly melancholy beauty, and British film pioneer Will Barker. I sometimes think research is one of life's most rewarding pastimes, especially if it leads to writing about the matter of your life's obsession. In the pipeline, apart from more regular reviewings, there's a chapter on *Under Capricorn* and *The Paradine Case* for a book on 'Hitchcock the moralist' ('Do you know anything about morality?' Gerie asked) and, believe it or not, the editor of a serious online journal asked me if I'd like to write a piece about Merle Oberon for a series on 'Beautiful women in the cinema'. Naturally, Merle was his first thought — as she would have been mine in a similar situation — and naturally I said yes.

It's good no longer to have to feel guilty about an obsession with the cinema; it's good no longer to have to bother too much with arcane theory to justify it; it's just good to have something so rewarding to do nearly every day of my life — almost as good as grandchildren and certainly better than the garden.